Your Divine Life

Angelic Guidance for the Ascension

CHRISTINA LUNDEN

Your Divine Life

ANGELIC GUIDANCE FOR THE ASCENSION

Outkirts Press, Inc.
Denver, Colorado

The opinions expressed in this manuscript are solely the opinions of the author and do not represent the opinions or thoughts of the publisher. The author has represented and warranted full ownership and/or legal right to publish all the materials in this book.

Your Divine Life
Angelic Guidance for the Ascension
All Rights Reserved.
Copyright © 2009 Christina Lunden
v4.0

Cover Photo © 2009 JupiterImages Corporation. All rights reserved - used with permission.

This book may not be reproduced, transmitted, or stored in whole or in part by any means, including graphic, electronic, or mechanical without the express written consent of the publisher except in the case of brief quotations embodied in critical articles and reviews.

Outskirts Press, Inc.
http://www.outskirtspress.com

ISBN: 978-1-4327-4122-8

Library of Congress Control Number: 2009927231

Outskirts Press and the "OP" logo are trademarks belonging to Outskirts Press, Inc.

PRINTED IN THE UNITED STATES OF AMERICA

DEDICATION

To my husband Dana: I wouldn't even be writing this book if it weren't for your love and support. I know we live a very different life because of my spiritual work. I realize the sacrifices you have made in order to make my work of serving and healing others possible. I pray that you know how very much I love and appreciate you. I cannot imagine being here on Earth at this time without you in my life. You have helped the Lord mold me into who I am today and even though it was painful at times, it has all been worth it. Thank you, my greatest love!

TABLE OF CONTENTS

INTRODUCTION 1
CHAKRAS 5
HEALING YOURSELF 15
FINALLY BREAKING THROUGH 27
FORGIVENESS THROUGH WHITE-WATER RAFTING .. 45
YOUR HIGHEST AND GREATEST LOVE NOW 55
ASCENSION SYMPTOMS 81
A KEY FOR YOUR HEART 87
LIVING WELL 91
REFRESHING YOUR SPIRIT 115
MATILDA 143
MICHAEL & EINSTEIN 149
FINAL THOUGHTS 155
SHORT ARCHANGEL CHAKRA PRAYER 158
FOR MORE INFORMATION ABOUT CHRISTINA 159

MY MISSION STATEMENT

To be an anointed Ambassador for the Lord. To serve by example and to share insight, wisdom and knowledge with those who come to me. With strength and power I convey truth through compassion and love; which brings peace, joy and hope.

ACKNOWLEDGEMENTS

Photography:

- Dana Lunden of Photos By Design www.PhotosByDesign1.com

Editors:

- Wendy Elwell of Conscious Creations www.consciouscreations.us

- Dianna Ford

MY PRAYER

"I thank you Lord, for Your *light* and Your perfect healing power that flows through me.

I come to you in prayer asking that you now fill my heart and my hands with Your healing love, wisdom, and encouragement and make me Your masterpiece for this child who is here today to be healed by You.

I ask Jesus to now stand with me and anoint me with His power to command healing and give me revelation knowledge.

And I ask for Saint Michael to now surround the reader and me with the protection of the whole armor of God.

We humbly accept these gifts of grace from You.

Thank you Lord! Amen."

"Ask, and it will be given to you; seek, and you will find; knock, and it will be opened to you. For everyone who asks receives, and he who seeks finds, and to him who knocks it will be opened."

~ Matthew 7:7- 8

INTRODUCTION

AS far back as I can remember I have been able to see visions and hear from Angels. I didn't realize when I was younger that they were Angels. I knew them as my friends. Whenever I saw Jesus He always had one of my "friends" on either side of Him. I talked to Him daily and thought everyone could see Him. I was told by a family member to stop speaking out loud about such things because others couldn't see Him the way I did. I prayed to have my abilities turned off because it didn't seem to fit in with my daily life. They went away and then after a few years, I started seeing and knowing things again which I couldn't possibly have known on the Earthplane. It was very hard being a child and not understanding how this could be so upsetting to people when it was so natural for me. After many years of denying my abilities I eventually decided to learn more about them. As I write this, I am now 26 years into this process of remembering who I am as a spiritual human being and I am grateful that I made that decision.

During this time of connecting to my spiritual side, I would ask a question about something I wanted to learn about and Jesus would name three scriptures and I would go read them as my answer. The majority of my communication with the Lord has been through Bible scripture. To my amazement, each time all three scriptures correlated with whatever question I was asking at the time.

Eventually I realized that my abilities were not just for me to keep to myself and I should no longer hide them. So I spent time in prayer asking what I was to do and received my answer. I was to work for the Lord with His Angels to guide and heal people who would then go out to serve by guiding and healing other people. I was going to be teaching and sharing with the *Lightworkers* and *Lightbearers*.

The scriptures I received at that time in reference to direction for my life's work were:

Go, stand in the temple and speak to the people all the words of this life. ~ Acts 5:20

Whoever therefore breaks one of the least of these commandments, and teaches men so, shall be called least in the kingdom of Heaven; but whoever does and teaches them, he shall be called great in the kingdom of Heaven. ~ Matthew 5:19-20

INTRODUCTION

But as it is written: "Eye has not seen, nor ear heard, nor have entered into the heart of man the things which God has prepared for those who love Him." But God has revealed them to us through His spirit. For the Spirit searches all things, yes, the deep things of God. ~ 1 Corinthians 2:9-10

And thus my work began. Even though my journey is with Jesus in my daily experiences, I do not teach or preach any one religion. I recognize and honor everyone's divine journey, as Jesus did while He walked the Earth. We are all going in the same direction to the same end; full remembrance of who we are as the Christ being or in other words...enlightenment. Sometimes we take different paths to get there. Through choices, at times in our many lives our paths are going to cross. My life journey has been to help and teach anyone with an open heart; regardless of what religion you chose for yourself in this life. It is an honor to help others make a stronger spiritual connection in a clearer way for themselves.

We are living at an amazing time in our many lives as spiritual human beings. We were born into the 3rd dimensional world where each Soul had situations and people brought to them according to their karma. We also were very controlled by our egos. Our lives were pretty well planned. There was not much we could do to alter our individual paths. In 2003, we changed our collective course on Earth and ascended to the 4th dimension. With this blessed ascension energy, we have had many unexpected changes in our lives. All karmic ties were severed and the ego has lost its power. Take a moment to look back at your own life around the year 2003. Did you have big changes in your life? I am excited to be sharing with many of you who want to learn as much as you can about the Ascension and learn how to utilize this new energy to the fullest extent.

In the 4th dimension, it is easier to manifest the life that you want by speaking it. Throughout these pages, I will be sharing with you insights, meditations, prayers and stories, both personal and from clients, to help you be in the perfect place to receive the most blessings. The ultimate goal of every Soul is to remember who they are as a piece of God. My goal for this book is to help you during this time of Ascension walk the easiest path, in the highest energy, having the most joyful time, until you remember.

It is an honor to share with your Soul during this very special time on Earth. I pray that you have eyes to see, ears to hear and an open heart to receive all that you are seeking today!

May you be blessed by your Angels,

Christina

www.CreatorMediator.com

CHAKRAS

WHEN I first started my spiritual work, I didn't even know what a chakra was. I was told by the Angels that I needed to learn about them so I could share prayers with people who were walking this incredible spiritual journey as it would help them along the way. Instead of teaching me like they had before by receiving the information spiritually, the Angels guided me to another person's work with chakras. Her name is Ambika Wauters. They told me they had already given her the information and there was no need to duplicate the teaching. I would just need to read the book, The Book of Chakras; Discover the Hidden Forces Within You and they, the Angels would guide me from there. I read every word of this book many, many times. Very simply put, the chakras are energy centers that contain our life force and are our connection to the "real" beings that we are. They follow our thoughts and actions. So if we are positive, the chakras would be active and open wide and our connection to Spirit would be strong. If we are negative, the chakras become weak and narrow. This can make us sick, depressed and feeling like we are alone.

The chakras are not in our physical body. They are in our aura. If you were visualizing them, you would see them a few inches away from your physical body with a cone of energy flowing out of your spine in front of you and behind you getting bigger and wider the further it goes. A normal chakra resonates about four inches away from the body. For someone who is active spiritually, they could expand this to six inches. *I would highly recommend Ambika Wauters book if you would like to know more detailed information about chakras as I am going to move on to what information the Angels gave me after reading the book myself.*

Since Ambika Wauters book was published in 2002 before the switch to the 4th dimension, it contains the seven 3rd dimensional chakras: the Root Chakra, the Sacral Chakra, the Solar Plexus Chakra, the Heart Chakra, the Throat Chakra, the Brow Chakra and the Crown Chakra. These are the chakras that we have had open to us for over 2,000 years of walking in 3rd dimensional energy.

With the arrival of the 4th dimension, we have been blessed with access to three more chakras. It's not that these are new chakras to our souls. It is that they have not been open and we were not able to access them consciously before. The first 4th dimensional chakra to open up to us was the Soul Star Chakra. This chakra resides about four feet above your head. The name Soul Star is a great description as it connects us to our Soul's *light*. It is the direct portal to our souls. With this chakra being open, you have more access to your spiritual abilities and power.

The next chakra to open was the High Heart Chakra. This chakra connects to the area under your throat where the thymus is located; at the indentation. This chakra opens when you are ready to work on lessons of compassion and non-judgment. Since it is so close to the throat chakra, it helps you speak with more truth, graciousness and integrity. Let me point out that everyone who has this chakra open will not speak with truth, graciousness and integrity. Just because a chakra is open doesn't mean they are accessing all the qualities that come with that chakra. The more the person is utilizing these qualities will enhance the strength and power of the chakra. If someone was consciously lying, the chakra's spin would slow down or the chakra would shut down if it was excessive. That is what happens to any chakra when people go against what energy the chakra connects us to. The more you are in alignment with the energy of that chakra, the faster and stronger it spins which in turn makes you more connected to your spiritual abilities.

The third new chakra that the 4th dimension has opened up for us is the Zeal Point Chakra. This is also sometimes called the Well of Dreams Chakra. This chakra resides behind the base of the neck. It is considered to be the opening to the mouth of God. When this chakra first opens up, there may be neck and shoulder pain. If you have unexplained neck and shoulder issues and you are somewhat new to your spiritual path, this may be opening for the first time. You can control the spin or flow of the chakra by placing your hand behind your neck; hold it about two inches away and ask your Angels to back the energy down to a slower spin. This should alleviate any pain that you are experiencing because of the chakra opening. The Zeal Point Chakra helps us connect to clearer information through our dreams. You can also channel clearer information when this is open. The Zeal Point Chakra is the final 4th dimensional chakra to open. It will not open until the Soul Star Chakra and High Heart Chakra have been open and balanced for a while. I say a while instead of a particular time frame since there is no time in Spirit and it depends on how quickly your soul integrates the information, lessons and energy.

To recap, you have three Earthplane chakras: Root Chakra, Sacral Chakra and Solar Plexus Chakra. Then you have one connecting chakra, the Heart Chakra. Then you have the spiritual chakras, the High Heart Chakra, Throat Chakra, Brow Chakra, Crown Chakra, Soul Star Chakra and the Zeal Point Chakra. That is three Earthplane chakras balancing the seven spiritual chakras! The higher you go on a spiritual level the harder the lower three chakras will be working to keep you balanced. Try to maintain a balance in all your chakras and not concentrate too much on any one.

Here is a guide to visualize where each chakra resonates with you. Think of a line going down the center of your body from top to bottom. We will move up this line starting with the Root Chakra:

<u>Root Chakra</u> - the bottom of your trunk in the center of your body, where your legs start

Sacral Chakra – just below your belly button

Solar Plexus Chakra - just above your belly button

Heart Chakra – this is in the center of your chest; not where Americans put their hand for the Pledge of Allegiance.

High Heart Chakra – just below the throat where the indentation is

Throat Chakra – middle of your throat

Brow Chakra - This is also called the Third Eye. It is in-between your eyebrows on the bridge of your nose

Crown Chakra – go to the middle of the top of your head, and then move your hand towards the back about an inch

Soul Star Chakra – this resonates above your head about 4 feet

Zeal Point Chakra – this is behind you at the base of your neck

One day, I noticed when I was reading the chakra book; a prayer was forming in my head. I wrote down the words and those words eventually became the first Archangel Chakra Prayer. At that time, in 2003, we were just becoming aware of the 4th dimensional energy. This Chakra Prayer will bless anyone in 3rd or 4th dimensional energy. I was told that saying this prayer would assist people in bringing in energy to enable them to hold the 4th dimensional energies easier. We recommend saying this prayer or some form of it every day to help you stay balanced and spiritually connected. (Note: For the High Heart Chakra, Archangel Tzadkiel's name is pronounced Zad-key-el.)

ARCHANGEL CHAKRA PRAYER

I call on Archangel Michael to assist me in opening and maintaining my Root Chakra. Thank you, Archangel Michael for helping me to stay grounded in this world. I thank you, for helping me walk on the easy path of my life, as I get closer to the fulfillment of my purpose. I thank you, Archangel Michael.

I call on Archangel Metatron to assist me in opening and maintaining my Sacral Chakra. Thank you, Archangel Metatron for helping me to recognize my physical and emotional needs. I call on you to assist me whenever I am out of balance. I thank you for reminding me to choose joy for each day of my life. I thank you, Archangel Metatron.

I call on Archangel Uriel to assist me in opening and maintaining my Solar Plexus Chakra. Thank you,

Archangel Uriel for reminding me to use my power. I call on you to help me remember to breathe. I am asking for you to strengthen my connection to the Source of all life. Each day with your help I strive to keep fear out of my thoughts. I thank you that I now understand who I truly am. I thank you, Archangel Uriel.

Breathe in deep

Pull in your naval as if to touch your spine

Breathe out, pushing all the air out

I call on Archangel Raphael to assist me in opening and maintaining my Heart Chakra. Thank you, Archangel Raphael for reminding me that God's love and *light* is a part of me as I am a part of Him. As I accept more of this love and *light*, I am filled to overflowing and I choose to share that *light* with others. I call on you to assist me to heal and move past anything that is not of the highest *light*. I thank you, Archangel Raphael.

I call on Archangel Tzadkiel to assist me in opening and maintaining my High Heart Chakra. Thank you, Archangel Tzadkiel for helping me to understand, to accept and to practice Universal love and compassion. I thank you that I am now open to following my heart's

guidance every day. I thank you, Archangel Tzadkiel.

Stay in your heart – feel the energy

Feel the strengthening of your connection to Spirit

I call on Archangel Gabriel to assist me in opening and maintaining my Throat Chakra. Thank you, Archangel Gabriel for reminding me to speak my truth and honor my needs. I call on you to help me know when to speak and when to listen. I choose now to see the truth, hear the truth, speak the truth, feel the truth...to be truth each day of my life. I thank you, Archangel Gabriel.

I call on the Holy Spirit to assist me in opening and maintaining my Brow Chakra. Thank You, Holy Spirit for assisting me with gaining spiritual knowledge, intuition and growing in the strength of the power that is rightfully mine. I call on You to remind me that the people I meet each day have a specific purpose for their life also. I recognize they are a part of the Divine; which makes them a part of me, as we are all One. I thank You, Holy Spirit.

I call on the Christ Light to assist me in opening and maintaining my Crown Chakra. Thank You, Christ Light for this permanent connection of *light* flowing through me in a stronger way each day. I now allow this *light* to heal every aspect of my soul. I call on

You to remind me to share this bright *light* with others each day as I walk through my life. I recognize that I am always connected to God and choose to walk in that *light* more consciously. I thank You, Christ Light.

I call on Enoch to assist me in opening and maintaining my Soul Star Chakra. Thank you, Enoch for helping me to focus my attention on the small, everyday things and to help me perform them with love. I now raise my awareness of quality and understanding on all levels. I now have access to the Divine blueprint of my life and I know what my potential and my purpose is. With your help, I strive to be a balanced spiritual being sharing love and *light* wherever I go. I thank you, Enoch.

I call on Archangel Chamuel to assist me in opening and maintaining my Zeal Point Chakra. You help me remember my dreams. You remind me that these visions have information that can help me. You teach me how to use this information in my daily life. I thank you, Archangel Chamuel.

Deep breath in

Breathe out

As you say the chakra prayers over time, it will be easy to recognize if a particular chakra is out of balance. Eventually you won't need to say all the words of the chakra prayer. You won't need to call in the Archangels for help with your chakras. Until that time, it is best to say the Archangel Chakra Prayer that gives the fullest explanation of what areas you might need to be working on in your life. These chakra prayers make you more consciously aware of what needs to be cleared in order to advance to the next spiritual level. That is what we are teaching you. We are empowering you to be the highest spiritual being you can be.

HEALING YOURSELF

I was walking on a treadmill at the gym one day and I heard a lady cough across the room while I was working out. I was saying my prayers so I decided to send her some healing *light* energy. After I was done, the Angels gave me this meditation that we can use to heal ourselves but then use the high energy that we are in to share that energy with everyone around the planet.

Please note, if you have had anything placed in your body or had anything removed, when you participate in this meditation, act as if it is still there and / or in perfect health. For instance, if you have had a hysterectomy when you say the part about your organs, it is important for you to feel complete and whole so that your body responds to you in the same way. Your physical body follows your emotional thoughts. If you think you are lacking because you are missing some part of your body, you will show signs of lack. It is possible to have a complete hysterectomy and not have to take any pills to correct your hormones if you have a belief that energetically everything is still intact. I pray this meditation is a blessing to you.

MEDITATION FOR CELLULAR HEALING AND SHARING HEALING *LIGHT* WITH THE WORLD

Sit or Lie down in a comfortable position

Take a deep breath in

Breathe out

State your own prayer to call in the highest energy available to you or state this prayer:

*"I thank the Universe for Your love and Your *light* as I call forth the highest Angels to bring me power, healing and *light* energy. I thank You for Your protection as I do so and I thank You that I am a clear and pure channel of this loving *light*. Amen."*

Take a deep breath and hold it 1 second…2 seconds…

Breathe out and hold it 1 second…2 seconds…

Take a deep breath and hold it 1...2...3...

Breathe out and hold it 1...2...3...

Take a deep breath and hold it 1...2...3...4...

Breathe out and hold it 1...2...3...4...

Continue to breathe calmly yet deeply.

State your intention to the Universe of what you would like to create for your life at this time...

(Intentions here)

Say this after you state your intentions, "Universe show me clear signs that you have heard me and that these things will be done."

You are now becoming one with the Universe.

Feel the *light* flowing in through your Crown Chakra and up through your Root Chakra, meeting at your Heart Chakra. This *light* energy flow is continuously pouring out of your Heart Chakra.

Take a deep breath in and hold it 1...2...3...

Breathe it out, and hold it out 1...2...3...

Deep breath in, hold it 1…2…3…

Breathe out, hold it 1…2…3…

Take a big, deep breath in, hold it 1…2…3…

Breathe out, hold it out 1…2…3…

Talking to your cells:

"Cells, I want you to start vibrating with the highest *light* energy you can hold."

Breathe

"Cells conform to the highest energy or remove yourself from my system with new, perfect cells replacing you."

"All is made right within my cells immediately."

Breathe

"My cells are in complete and perfect balance."

Deep breath in, sealing this intention.

Breathe out

Talking to your organs:

"Organs, I want you to function with the highest *light* energy you can hold."

"All is made right within my organs immediately."

Breathe

"My organs are now in complete and perfect balance."

Take a deep breath in, sealing this intention.

Breathe out.

Speaking to the arteries:

"Veins and arteries, I want you to function and flow with the highest *light* energy you can hold."

"My veins and arteries are now flowing smoothly and perfectly throughout all of my body."

Breathe.

"My veins and arteries have just been cleansed by the highest *light*."

"All is made right within my veins and arteries immediately."

Take a deep breath in, sealing this intention with *light*.

Breathe out.

Now state any specific part of your body that you want to pour this powerful *light* energy into.

"My _____ is now made perfect, whole and complete with the highest *light*."

Knowing this and believing this, take a deep breath in… breathing in that *light* and breathing out anything left that is not of the highest *light* energy in your body.

"All is made right throughout my entire body."

Visualize a cross of *light* within a circle of *light*, sealing and protecting the changes that you have created.

Breathe

Take a few moments to feel your body responding to what you have said.

Feel the power of what you have accomplished.

Now take this *light* that is flowing through you and send it to the room that you are now in and to every living thing in it.

See the *light* filling the room.

Continue to consciously breathe.

Now send this *light* throughout the building that you are in. See the *light* flowing through your heart and expanding into the building.

Send this *light* to the street or neighborhood you are currently in. See the *light* encompassing the entire area.

Where there is *light*, no dark can be.

Take a deep breath in and allow more *light* to flow in through your Crown Chakra and up through your Root Chakra and out of your heart.

Now send this strong, loving *light* even further, surrounding the city that you are in.

Nothing can stop this *light* from encompassing and filling the city.

Now take this *light* and send it to the state that you are in.

YOUR DIVINE LIFE

You can visualize an outline of your state and see the *light* engulfing it or you can simply say your state's name.

The *light* must go wherever you send it.

See the *light* infusing into the dirt and flowing upward into the sky.

Take a deep breath in

Breathe out

Now send this *light* to your country.

See the country outline and infuse it with this loving *light* that is flowing through you right now.

Take a deep breath in

Breathe out.

Send this powerful, strong, loving *light* to all the continents and land masses of Mother Earth by saying the continents names: "Antarctica, South America, North America, Europe, Africa, Asia and Australia."

By stating these names, know the *light* is infusing these places at this time.

Now send this *light* to the waters that surround the continents and sustain us. Every stream, river, lake, and ocean is renewed at this moment with the highest *light* energy.

Now take a deep breath in…hold it

Breathe out…hold it

Now pull your vision out into space

And look at Mother Earth

See her completely surrounded in this *light* that you are channeling from the Source.

Breathe and hold the intention that *light* is healing all at this very moment.

There are no judgments on where you think it is needed.

You are the channel, allowing this powerful, loving *light* energy to flow through you.

Place your hand in front of your heart. Placing love, *light* and peace into your open hand. Breathe it into everything everywhere now.

Say: "The Breath of God delivers love, *light* and peace through me now to everyone and everything."

Feel complete.

Now say these affirmations: "I AM peace. I AM *light*. I AM love."

Take a deep breath in, integrating this energy.

Breathe out.

Believe you have touched all things with this meditation. Change has occurred by your presence, by your *light*.

Take a deep breath in and hold it

And breathe out and release.

SUE'S STORY OF DIVINE TIMING

DURING one of Christina's teaching phone calls, our focus was to call in our Heavenly Angels to assist us on our earthly journey. And she explained that part of our purpose here on Earth is to be an Angel to those whose path crosses ours and vice versa. Right after the teaching, my daughter and I were in a rush walking through a parking lot in the snow and slush trying to get to my car. We had to go to an appointment and then back again before a store was to close. We had 45 minutes to do all of this. As we walked to our car, I looked behind me and I thought I saw some guy on the ground trying to pull something out from under his front tire. Then I heard a weak cry for help. We ran to the car to see an elderly woman lying in the slush with her head wedged in the front wheel well of the car. She had fallen when she didn't see the curb because it had been covered with snow. When she fell down she hit her head on the car. Her cane lay on the ground next to her. I reached behind her shoulders to pull her out from under the car. With the help of two other ladies, we slowly raised this frail woman to her feet and moved her to the sidewalk and then slowly into the building. I was behind her the whole time talking her through each step to make sure she was okay. One of the other ladies asked me if I was a nurse. Puzzled for a minute, I said, "No, just someone passing by in time to help someone else in need." We finally made it into a store. The old woman's coat was soaking wet. We sat her down and she quickly turned to look at me. For that moment, when she said, "Thank you, thank you, thank you!" my eyes filled with tears as I knew that it was a divine Angel moment. I felt so fortunate to have been there to help her. I used that opportunity as a teachable moment to talk to my 16 year old daughter about compassion and caring about others. I honestly don't remember the woman's face right now but I do remember the overwhelming feeling I had when she said, "Thank you!"

While I sometimes struggle with other issues in my life, I can't even begin to quantify the blessing I received from that experience. I know all that I am learning through Christina helps to me bring me closer to true love and compassion.

FINALLY BREAKING THROUGH

BEFORE you begin reading this chapter, take a moment to write down a list of things in your life that you would like to see happen or changed. Perhaps they are things that you want for your life but until now have not seen signs of it manifesting or it is not manifesting quickly enough. Be bold and place your intent strongly to the Universe that you want to receive what you are stating for your life. You deserve the things of your dreams or you wouldn't be having them. Why wait for it? Let's work together to create the change that you want in your life, for your family and for our world. Later, we will call forth the Angels to get working on manifesting these things you write down. You can have as big a breakthrough as you can believe for, so write your list and let's get the things to you that you deserve!

The Angels have given us the following exercise to help break through the barriers and fears that we have holding us back. This includes fears and thoughts that we don't deserve to have the things that we desire. They shared with me that you would not have a desire in your heart if you were not able to fulfill it. If it is in your heart, you can have it. If it is in your brain, then that may not be so. But, if you feel it in your heart that this is something that you truly want then what we do today will work through your chakras to help you manifest those things. This will happen because you will be firmly balanced between Heaven and Earth. We are supposed to be balanced between Heaven and Earth because we are spiritual beings having a physical human existence. We are not supposed to be more on the Earth, or all on the Earth, or even all in spirit. Right now, since we are all residing on the Earthplane, we are supposed to be in both places at the same time and we are supposed to be maintaining that balance. Depression, fears, all things which hold us back, show us that we are unbalanced. These chakra prayers may seem like they're not as powerful as they really are because you've said them ten times or more. But the Angels say that they are just as powerful as the first time you stated them. Keep your intentions high. You can walk through your life and have your dreams and desires fulfilled.

Now we are going to walk through each chakra; having you put *light* into each of them using your hands. You visualize it in this way, but we want you to know the *light* is actually coming from your heart. For our purposes of placing intentions into each chakra it is easier to direct it with your hand. In essence, the *light* is flowing from your heart to your hand to your chakras.

Root Chakra – Place your dominant hand two to three inches above your Root Chakra. Take three long, slow, deep breaths and visualize putting *light* into that area. Feel the *light* getting stronger with each breath. Take your time.

Sacral Chakra – Place your hand two to three inches above your Sacral Chakra. Take three long, slow, deep breaths and visualize putting *light* into that area. Feel the *light* getting stronger with each breath.

Solar Plexus Chakra – This time we are going to do it a little different. Breathe in, holding your hand two to three inches out from your Solar Plexus Chakra. Breathe out. This time when you take a deep breath in we want you to hold it. Then push all the air out while pulling your belly button in as if you were going to have it touch your back.

Heart Chakra – Take a deep breath in, holding your hand two to three inches away from your heart center. See the golden white *light* flowing from your hand. As you breathe out, make a circle with your hand as if you were massaging your heart. Take another deep breath in, keep massaging, and breathe out. The Angels want you to hold there for a few seconds. Stop massaging. Imagine that the *light* is going all the way through your heart and all the way through your back. This very strong *light* is energetically cleansing every aspect of you; emotionally and physically, while it also is helping to raise your energy spiritually. Take another deep breath in, hold it, and breathe out.

Before we move on to the Throat Chakra, I am going to divide the group. Those people that are or want to be spiritual teachers or those that feel that your voice helps to heal others; I want you to move your fingers back and forth as if you were rubbing something off of your Throat Chakra. Also, imagine that the *light* is coming up through your hand in waves. Everyone else you can raise your energy by putting your hand in front of your throat but you do not have to move your hand back and forth.

<u>Throat Chakra</u> – Everyone take a deep breath in and breathe out. Take another deep breath in. Now send that *light* out to the Universe while you breathe out. Take a deep breath in, hold it, and breathe out.

<u>Brow Chakra</u> – Everyone is going to be doing the same thing for this chakra. Just like we did the massaging for the heart, you are going to be using the palm of your hand, not your fingers, to massage two to three inches out from your Brow Chakra. By doing this, you will be opening or enhancing your spiritual sight and becoming more open to your intuition. Start massaging and take a deep breath in and breathe out. Repeat this for two more deep breaths. On the final breath, take a deep breath in, sending the *light* from the palm of your hand into your Brow Chakra. Hold your breath, still massaging with your palm and breathe out. Release anything and everything that was stuck there that needed to be released. It is gone. Now just hold your hand in front of your Brow Chakra. Breathe one more time in and out.

Crown Chakra — The Crown Chakra resides two to three inches above your head. Place your palm over the middle part of your head and then move it back one to two inches. Take a deep breath in and breathe out. Repeat this two more times. Now, imagine the *light* is flowing from Heaven through your hand into your Crown Chakra flowing all the way down, and then breathe out. Take another deep breath in and breathe out.

Now run your hand from your Crown Chakra down the front of your body in front of each and every chakra, holding one to two seconds over every chakra. Feel them. Can you feel a difference from when you started this exercise? Can you feel each chakra energetically? Don't worry, over time you will notice a difference, even if you can't now.

Now with your hand make a huge cross of *light* over your body. Starting above your head bring your hand straight down the front of your body and then across from shoulder to shoulder. Imagine that this cross is made of white *light* flowing from your hand. Then surround that cross of *light* with a circle of *light* by drawing a big circle in front of you. That is sealing your intentions for what you just did. You have now got the Archangels, the Holy Spirit and the Christ light helping you to maintain the opening of your chakras.

Now you have a lot of energy moving through you. So for the next thirty seconds, I want you to put this book down, stand up and move your entire body. Shake your hands, your legs, your arms.

If you are sitting down and cannot get up, I want you to move as much of your body as you possibly can. Take a deep breath in and breathe out. How do you feel?

It's important for you to recognize what you are going through and seeing these situations and issues from a soul aspect. Also, it is important for you to understand what you are capable of on the Earthplane. You do deserve all of the things you are asking for or are afraid to ask for. I was asking the Angels how we could break through all of this and that is how this exercise evolved. I hope you are feeling a difference and this teaching and exercise is blessing you.

The Angels have said that we are a piece of God, a thought of God. We feel the separateness of God, although God does not. Since He is a part of us and we are a part of Him, He can speak to us. He speaks to us through our cells, through our intuition, through the Angels, through the Holy Spirit. He is speaking to you. He hasn't been ignoring any one of us. It's impossible for Him to ignore any one of us because we are a part of Him. What I've learned from helping others is that if you're not hearing Him, you are not asking questions or you are not stopping long enough to listen. If you have a really important question that you need answered, you need to take the time to put yourself in a quiet space to make it easier to receive the answer. Especially if you are new to your spiritual path or if you aren't skilled yet at knowing when Spirit is talking to you. If you are at work and you need an answer

FINALLY BREAKING THROUGH

right then, go to the restroom, go out by yourself, go to your car, wherever you can be alone and call forth the Angels to give you an answer to your question. To do this, take at least three long, slow, deep breaths to make your spiritual connection stronger.

You have to believe that you can make this spiritual connection. If you are walking around saying, "Oh, I can never hear the Angels," or, "Christina can hear the Angels but I can't," then you need to realize that you won't be able to until you change your thoughts. I can hear the Angels because I have made it a point to connect to the Angels every day for years. I have worked long and hard at this. It wasn't easy for me but you have it so much easier than I did because we are in a much higher resonation and dimension now. And that makes less "space' so to speak between you and Spirit so it is easier to connect now. If you are saying something negative about your spiritual abilities, you need to change your thoughts or you won't progress spiritually. There is nothing stopping you from doing it except you! Every time you can't seem to hear from the Angels or hear from God, instead of getting frustrated, say out loud, "I can!" State what you want instead of what you don't want in your life. You are creating your life by your thoughts and your words. Believe with all your heart that you can. It will take time to reverse the energy from the negatives that you have been saying but it will change quicker the stronger you believe you can do it. I believe you can hear from your Angels. I believe that every single person reading these words can hear from their Angels. There is no reason why you cannot, if you want to.

When you say your affirmations, we recommend using the words, "I AM." Saying "I AM" is very powerful because it is a name of God. You are calling forth your piece of God to help you receive whatever you are affirming. Some examples are: "I AM now hearing from my Angels." "I AM now walking in the true power that I deserve." "I AM now receiving that raise." "I AM now receiving that job." Put a capitalized "I AM" in your affirmations and say them with power, like you mean it.

It is important to understand that the Angels are just messengers. I am just a messenger. Other people you go to for spiritual answers are just messengers. The important part is that you get the message! And that message is coming from inside of you. Did you know that you have every answer to every question you will ever ask, inside of you? Well, you do. You are a piece of God and God is answering you through His messengers. My job is to help you connect to the Divinity within yourself. When you connect with that, you will have comfort, peace, love, joy, abundance and so much more. Until you believe that you can reach that level, I am here for you to be able to help you walk through the situations that come up in your life. I am also here for another level of people that want to teach and serve others. I am here to help them start walking in their true power of what they can do. We need more people doing this kind of service. We need more people connecting to the *light* and pulling this energy into the world and not having it sit over our heads in Heaven. Because of the ascension, it is possible in our lifetimes to have Heaven on Earth but it is up to each one of us to create it.

You are a strong, powerful *light*. I want you to know how beautiful you are and the power you really have. You just have to flip the switch in your head from telling you that you do not deserve. It is important to move through your lesson of worthiness so you can feel that you deserve to do whatever it is you have been called to do. To do this, you need to stop listening to your ego, which will decrease its strength over you.

An amazing thing happened with one of the people that I love dearly. She had wonderful faith to win the lottery, get a job, get a new car, etc. She had faith but also over the years she had proven she could get anything she prayed for. I found out she wouldn't play the lottery because she knew she would win and in her mind that would be taking abundance away from someone else. In her case, she went to the opposite extreme of this lesson and was withholding from herself. She was sacrificing her desires. The Angels had to tell her that she needed to get back in balance; extremes are not good. They explained to her if she was blessed then she could bless others in a much bigger way. If she won the lottery, then she could share that with others that would never be in that position. She needed to be okay with feeling deserving that she could have those things, too. So, there are two sides to this deserving lesson.

Once you understand that you do deserve better than you have been allowing yourself to receive, you will be in a much better position to help others. Your heart will be open and radiate a wonderful *light* and people will migrate towards you to let you serve them. That is what most of us are doing at this time. We only have a few more things to learn for ourselves. And the rest of the time, we want to share our knowledge and wisdom with others to help them advance as well. Some of you may say, "Well, I am not in a position now to serve others." We are all in a position to serve others. We all have *light* that we shine every single moment of every day. Whether it is a *light* the size of a pen or a lighthouse that shines all the way around twenty-four hours a day, you have *light* to share with everyone you come in contact with each day just by being you.

We all serve while we are on the Earthplane. I have talked with some people whose only job while on Earth is to pray. They pray whenever they are guided by Spirit to pray. Sometimes they don't even know what they are praying for. The Angels use them because they are great prayer warriors who are able to assist unknown people and unknown situations day or night.

There are some people that bless the land every time their foot falls on the Earth no matter where they are. Sometimes, they are sent to certain parts of the country, to certain parts of the world to live or visit. It may not be a place that their heart really wanted to go but ultimately they knew that was where they were needed to be. They are serving us because they are holding the energy in that part of the world to help maintain balance for Mother Earth.

There are people who are strictly here to do regular jobs like school teachers, administrators, lawyers, accountants, trash collectors, etc. They are perfectly knowledgeable, wise spiritual teachers who look like they are not doing anything spiritual. They are sharing their *light* with people that some of us would never come in contact with. And they are the ones helping us through Earthplane situations for our highest and best and helping Mother Earth. People who are these special souls can sometimes feel that they are not doing anything to make a difference. But they are! Bless them when they cross your path. Pray for them to have the strength to do these jobs. Even if it looks like you are not walking in what you would think you are capable of spiritually, the Angels and I want you to know you are still sharing your *light*.

Now look over the list that you prepared at the beginning of this chapter. You and I are going to call what you want forth now. I will be with you in Spirit holding your hand, no matter when you do this, no matter how many times you do this exercise. There is no time and space in Spirit and I am agreeing to be there for you. You can have these things. If you aren't sure you deserve what you have written down, please be open to believing that you do deserve better than what you have now, if just for this exercise. We can always use more than what we have now. If you already have plenty of money, you can have more and you can use that money to be a blessing to others. You can have more love, more peace, more of whatever it is that your heart desires. There is no lack in Spirit.

Hold your list in front of your heart. Take a deep breath in and breathe it out. Visualize *light* coming down from Heaven through your Crown Chakra and up from Mother Earth through your Root Chakra. Imagine this *light* meets at your heart and flows out of it. The *light* then goes into your piece of paper which you are holding in front of your heart. State out loud with strong intention:

"I AM calling forth my highest Angels, the Archangels, the Holy Spirit and the Christ Light to bring forth all that I deserve, all that I desire. I pray that You are now bringing to life every single word that is written on my paper and even those I have yet to write. I thank you that I am joining hands with Christina, standing in agreement that each and every one of these things will manifest immediately for me now!"

Take a deep breath. Feel the *light* coming from your heart. Breathe out. There is no time in Spirit. The Universe is now moving on your behalf if you did this exercise and believed. Take another deep breath in. It is a strong energy that is manifesting these things for you now. Breathe out. When you feel complete, you can put your piece of paper down. You can throw it away, burn it, whatever you want, because the words are in Spirit right now.

In your own way, I want you to take a few moments and thank the Universe, the Angels, the Lord, all of the energies joining together to see you get your breakthrough. Bless everyone who is in agreement with you and thank them for making your dreams and your desires come true for you. Yes, even before it gets here. That shows you have faith and believe you deserve these things. Thank you, Thank you, and Thank you!

I wanted to go over briefly how you can connect with your Angels. Even if you have never done this before on your own, you are in perfect energy to do so now after reading this chapter. So if you were unsuccessful in the past, try again now. You have a lot of Angels with you right now waiting to help you more consciously.

It is easier to ask the Angels questions if they are already written down. You might want to take a moment to do that, leaving space for you to write the answers you receive from them.

When you are ready, we always start with a breath. Breathing is very, very healing. We breathe very shallow during the day and night so the deep breathing gives our physical bodies a chance to rejuvenate and heal. It balances us between Heaven and Earth, where we should be. And it also makes our connection to our Angels easier and stronger.

To start, take a few deep breaths, calling forth your Angels by simply saying you want to talk with your highest Angels. Remember to add a statement about your time with the Angels being protected by stating something like, "I AM protected!" You can also say, "I'm a clear and pure Channel."

Or you can use my prayer given to me by the Angels:

"I thank You, Lord for Your love and Your *light* as I call forth the highest Angels to bring information that is clear, helpful and useful for my life today. I thank You for Your protection as I do so. I thank You, that I AM a clear and pure channel of love and *light*. Amen."

Now start with your first question, which should already be written down. Read the first question and write down whatever comes to mind first, whether you see it, hear it, know it, whatever. Don't analyze what you receive. This is very important. The answer may be a word, a picture, a statement. Just describe whatever it is. Stay with that question until you stop receiving an answer. Then go right to the next question. And so forth. At the end, thank your Angels. That will disconnect the energy. Then you can go back and logically read over your answers.

The reason the Angels don't want you to analyze the information until you are completely done with your questions is because they want you to maintain that spiritual connection. It is easy to break that connection if you go back fully into your logical mind. After you are complete with asking your questions and you read your answers, the answers may not seem so significant. But if look at your questions and answers the next morning, you will feel the power in the answers. It might be pretty stunning. Have faith in yourself. You can get answers from your Angels. I have faith in you.

Now the Angels are saying that they want me to thank you for allowing them to share with you. They are bowing to you, honoring you for what you have done by opening your heart to receive all that you deserve. It is an honor for them to work with you, share with you and serve you; especially when you end up sharing that *light* with other people. Here is a prayer that I came up with to thank them:

"I want to thank all of the Angels for coming forth. Thank You, Lord for all of the blessings that I have received and for those that are now coming. I thank You for reminding me that I AM deserving and helping me to move past the barriers that I have allowed to remain in place for so long. I AM open and ready to now receive the blessings of my desires and the fulfillment of my purpose. I AM not waiting anymore. I AM going to do even more for You, more for Mother Earth, more for the Universe, and more in my lifetime. I thank You so much."

The Angels are saying that they want to speak directly to you now. During this time, be open to accepting the blessings being offered to you. Whenever they are speaking to you through my channeling, it is a perfect time for healing, so if you need a physical or emotional healing state your intention out loud now to be healed. This can be a powerful time for you if your heart is open.

"Greetings, we are Raphael and Gabriel. We are here to assist you walking forward. We see those things that you are struggling with and we wish to show you that you can receive these things, for they are already in process. Breathe deeply. Those things that you

placed on your paper and in your heart, visualize yourself walking in that energy achieving those desired things. Feel the energy of your joy and your happiness. Are you speaking before a group of a thousand, perhaps five thousand? Are you singing? Are you dancing? Are you playing music? Are you healing? Are you raising your children with the highest energy? Are you enjoying the most wonderful marriage? Are you seeing the Angels with your spiritual sight? Whatever it is that you have asked and stated these things are coming to you now. Feel the happiness and the joy and the great expectations. Having these emotions will help speed up the process to your receiving the things you have asked for. This energy that you feel is faith and trust. You are strong powerful beings and you are just now tapping into a small part of who you really are. Our work is just beginning with you. We have joined with you at this time to assist you as you assist the Universe in the Ascension.

There is no good and bad. There are view points. There is *light* and there is unenlightened. You are blessed that you have connected to this higher energy. There are some that never will in this lifetime. There is much excitement on the other side in the many dimensions that keep watch over this Earthplane. There are many that will be joining you and are working with you. They have waited for this day for a long time.

Those that are requesting sight to see things spiritually, we ask that you continually state in a positive manner: "I can see! I now see the unseen!" And if you want to hear spiritually, state, "I now hear what cannot be heard!" And if you want to Channel you can affirm, *"I now speak unspoken words!"*

We are here to assist you in all that you do. Remember that if you find yourself struggling again. At that time remember to breathe. It is such a simple thing and many walking this higher path do not remember to take deep breaths. We ask that you call forth the highest energies available to you and that you cover yourself with protection. And we will be there for you immediately.

Your *lights* are shining brighter than they ever have. There are *lights* coming from your heads going upwards and downwards into your physical bodies and all of your chakras have *lights* shining out of them. It is a beautiful sight to see!

We ask that you continue to breathe deeply, relax and enjoy the energy, this most healing energy that is being brought forth for those things that you wish to move past physically and emotionally. You do not need them any longer. We are here for you. You may call on us any time. There are many here to assist you. You are never alone. All you need to do is call us forth. We are leaving now, but we are never far."

FORGIVENESS THROUGH WHITE-WATER RAFTING

I would like to share this personal story with you about the power of forgiveness. I was guided by the Angels to buy the book, <u>Beyond Jabez</u>. At that time, I didn't really want to read it but the Angels told me that this book was going to be very helpful to me. The book was a blessing and what it taught me was to open up and pray to do more, to be more, to expand my territory which would put me in a position to help more people. It was such an incredible feeling after praying that prayer, at least for a short while.

Then things started going wrong all around me. Someone graciously sent me a virus, the My Doom Virus. This happened just after I had upgraded my computer and after I put in a new CD program to allow me to make CD's of my teachings. This would be my third computer crash of the year. Then I had to drop AOL as my internet service because some of my emails were not reaching people. I was having so much trouble getting my emails out and all AOL would tell me was to have all of my clients sign up with them and then there wouldn't be a problem. So bye bye AOL. Right after I dropped AOL, none of my clients that had AOL could receive my incoming emails. This was really frustrating! My computer is my lifeline to communicating with my clients! Then the Angel teaching by phone that night had static on the line. I asked everyone to take a moment to help clear the phone line. The intention worked but I had to get the phone company out the next day to see what was going on. The phone guy said there was a bunch of bees in the phone box and they had eaten through the phone line. The line was barely holding together. Within a day or two the phone line would have split in two. If I don't have a phone, I can't talk to clients and do my work. At the same time two of our children were graduating; one from high school and one from college. We also had two birthdays and if that wasn't enough we had a huge family fight. What made it all more confusing was that I had just prayed to be more, do more and to expand my territory. What was going on?

After the graduations, we were planning to take a family vacation to the North Carolina Mountains. I really needed the vacation! Not discounting the rest of the frustrating things that had happened, but the family issues really hurt me. I was struggling with what had happened saying to the Angels, "This isn't fair. I try to walk in truth. I try to be a good person. I don't understand why I keep being in these hurtful situations!" I don't think I was asking the right questions because all I heard back from the Angels was, "We love you. Breathe and feel peace." And other wonderful little statements that the Angels are known to say. That just made me angry. I needed help. I said, "Okay guys, this is really difficult and I am very angry. I don't know how to keep my balance here. I really need some help!" And I didn't hear an answer. I thought the trip was going to help and eventually it did however not in the way that I was expecting.

We ended up going to North Carolina with only half of our family. The only time I saw the Angels during the trip was in our cottage bedroom. They were standing like sentinels posted at the doors and windows, but this was different because they were facing away from me. I remember thinking that it was odd to see them that way but then I just forgot all about it.

One of the days, we went on a shuttle bus to go whitewater rafting. It was the first time that I have ever fully paid attention to the safety instructions. When we got to the river, the Angels kept telling me that I was going to get wet. I didn't believe them. Silly me! Everything was wonderful; the water, the sun and the relaxing way we were floating down the river. It was beautiful. Halfway through the trip the rafting guide asked us if we wanted to swim in an eddy, a calm pool area of the river. I laughingly said out loud that I was too old to swim in cold water. And immediately an Angel replied, "It doesn't matter because you are going to get wet anyway." Three different times I heard this. But I still didn't go swimming. I didn't believe the Angels. At that time, I did ask if I could loosen my safety vest because it was really tight. Our guide advised against it because she said if it got wet, it might just come right off of me. I left the vest the way it was.

Class I rapids are like ripples in your bathtub when you get in. They go up from there to Class VI which is unrunnable. There were going to be four Class IV's on this trip. She said that usually the water wasn't this rough but there had been some rain the night before in the mountains and when it does that it makes the river downstream swell.

The first half of the trip, we were preparing for these Class IV's. And we were doing well as a group. Everyone was listening to our guide and doing exactly what she said. She clearly explained what was going to happen and what each of us needed to do while going through each of these Class IV rapids. She then told us that three of them were going to be one right after the other. She showed us where they were in front of us and kept circling giving us last minute instructions.

Going down the very first Class IV rapid, the boat got caught and was being shifted right to left. The guy in front of me fell into the boat. With the next wave shift, without his body weight holding onto my foot, I got violently ejected from the raft. There was nothing I could do. It all happened so fast. I heard someone screaming while I was flipping through the air. I found out later, it was me. I went down the third Class IV rapid backwards with my feet going over my head. I couldn't come up for air. I remember not struggling, which probably saved my life. I remember thinking,

"I wish I had a camera." And then thinking how odd that was to have a thought like that. The water was so clear and everything was going in slow motion. I had my eyes open the whole time and I could see my body being pulled all over the place like a rag doll. I had no control over anything. However, I was calm, totally calm. Then I had another thought about being thankful the guide had not loosened my vest when I asked. If she had, I would have slipped right out of the very thing that was eventually going to get me back up to the air. I was under for what seemed like minutes. But not once did I panic. When I finally came up, I was so far away from the raft. I followed all the safety instructions that I had just watched on the bus…put your toes out of the water; point your feet downstream, etc. I wasn't worried.

When I finally got back in the raft, I saw everyone was panicking. "We thought you were dead. You didn't come up. We didn't know what was going on." And here I was still fine even though I did notice my heart was beating very fast, probably from the lack of oxygen. I sarcastically said to the Angels, "Thank you guys for telling me!" And they replied, "We did but you didn't want to believe us." The rafting guide was very apologetic. She said that had never happened in her raft before. I learned then that they got caught in a rapid reversal and were getting pounded by the water while being stuck on some rocks. They had to extricate themselves from that before they were able to move down to where I had come up.

Now I will explain the reason for sharing this story with you. Remember I had been through so much that month. I was definitely feeling sorry for myself. I was so worried about not being able to connect with my clients through phone sessions or email because of the computer and phone issues I had experienced. I finally realized while I was under the water getting thrown around that I had gotten slammed so many times in so many ways that month that I had finally surrendered. The easiest way to have dealt with the My Doom virus would have been by just getting someone to fix my computer; not to get upset about it. Then I could have dealt with the phone line issue the same way. That is the highest and best way to deal with life situations that come up. Just deal with it. You don't have to have chaotic feelings about the situation. You don't have to get angry. You don't have to get frustrated. We can choose to do that but you may have noticed from your own experiences, it makes things worse!

Some of you are in the same "raft" as me in that we don't have a lot of Earthplane support to help us while we are walking this path of remembering who we are. We have to walk this path while understanding the only sure support we will receive is from Spirit. I am being guided to remind you that we are in that position because we can do it ourselves; we are strong enough.

The other thought I had when I was down under the water was there were no Angels there. There was no one spiritually saying to me, "You are going to be okay." There was no one that spoke anything during that time because I was okay and I was strong enough to make it through that. It would have been so much worse if I was struggling and fighting the current. I could have drowned. I saved my energy because I trusted what the rafting guides had told me that I would eventually come up to the surface if I followed their instructions. And I trusted God that if it was my time to go, then I was going to see Him. "To be absent from the body is to be present with the Lord" is something I learned a long time ago. This statement has helped me rid myself of the fear of death. If it wasn't my time to die, then I had faith that I was going to be fine and I would come up when the conditions were right. And everything did work out and I was fine.

Except, I still felt anger towards some of the people because of what situations had occurred during the month. The human side of me felt justified in having the anger because I felt I had not done anything to anyone. I had analyzed the situation over and over in my head. To me it was unjust how I was being treated time and time again in situation after situation. Because of this I was about to get a spiritual spanking!

During the trip, with the exception of the time when the Angels told me I was going to get wet, they were silent; silent in an unusual way. I thought the Angels were giving me a break. When you hear as much as I do, it can get quite noisy. So not hearing was kind of like a nice break, if it had been for the right reasons. I didn't have dreams at night. I wasn't travelling through the dimensions. I wasn't being taught or shown things by the Angels. I wasn't doing any of the normal things I do.

Before we had left for the trip I had asked to see deer. In the past when I have done this, I have been able to connect with many different animals. It was always a fun way to connect with nature during my vacations. Well, it didn't happen. My husband saw a deer but I didn't. I started asking, "Where are you, Angels?" And there was no reply. It was then that I knew something was off. And I remembered the Angels being posted at my bedroom door with their backs to me since the beginning of our vacation. I started to get nervous and asked, "What is going on?" The Angels replied, "You have unforgiveness in your heart." I said, "What!?" They replied, "You have not forgiven them." And I said, "But I am mad." They replied, "Yes, you are and you need to get over it." And I started to argue, "But…." And I came up in my mind with all of these justifications for why I had a right to be mad. What I recognized is that I had a free will choice to stay angry and feel justified with what was going on between me and these people. And with that I was maintaining a negative spiritual tie with them. Did I really want that? Or did I want things to get better? What I didn't realize at the time was that my unwillingness to forgive would block my spiritual abilities and connection. That had never happened to me before. I have always steadily increased in my abilities. Until this I had never been blocked spiritually. It was a shock. I decided right then that my holding anger towards these people was not worth the price I was paying.

The Angels then explained further that when you are just learning to connect spiritually, you are learning truth, learning to deal with things from your past, you have more leeway with what you are responsible for because of your knowledge level. But when you increase in knowledge, you carry more responsibility. And with the responsibility comes consequences for anything that goes against the positive spiritual path you are on. I now know from what I have been through, forgiveness does block your spiritual development. It does take hold of a part of your heart and that part is not accessible to Spirit's love or *light* until you release it. I realized I needed to forgive these people even though it wasn't easy. And I did completely forgive them at that time and then I forgave myself for my part in our interactions.

Immediately, I felt like a huge weight had been lifted off me. I recognize I no longer have that negative tie to those people and I knew that I could choose to deal with them again or not. Forgiving them does not mean you have to put those people back in your life or in a position where they will do these same things to you. But it is important for you to take the higher road and not let anyone hold you back from the highest you can have. I know in my heart, those people didn't even know what I was going through. I was the only one carrying the burden about my feelings. I knew that I did want a relationship with them, not the same we had but a more loving one. I knew it would take time but I was willing to wait as long as it took.

Moving ahead a few years, everything has been forgiven on both sides now. I am so happy with the higher level of relationship that we have moved to as a family. Even though it took a while, my prayers forgiving them, forgiving myself and asking that we move past this into a more loving relationship were answered.

I didn't realize what the effect of praying the Prayer of Jabez would have for me. It opened up my consciousness to areas of my ego that still needed to be purged of lower energies. In this case, it showed me where I was still having thoughts of always being right and not looking at other people's perspectives. I wasn't willing at that time to look at the bigger picture. Since I have gone through this, I have recognized the price I will pay for holding onto unforgiveness. And because of that it has been much easier for me to forgive immediately all situations and keep my heart open for the higher love and *light* to flow through me.

YOUR HIGHEST AND GREATEST LOVE NOW

IN this Angel teaching on Love, we are going to prepare you to open up your heart and accept a greater, higher love in your life. This is even if you are currently in a love relationship. In either case, whether you are in a relationship or are single, you have the opportunity to change the vibration of love in your life now.

The Angels reminded me right before I started writing this that I have Peace Lilies in my office, where I do my phone Soul Sessions and teachings. The reason that my friend was guided to bring me a Peace Lily was because it has the ability to transmute negative energy into *light* and love. Of course, you might have to take this on faith but I know spiritually it works. I did do some research when I got the Peace Lilies and on the internet I found out that one Peace Lily will clear an 8 x 10 room. If you are having difficulties at work or in your relationship and you would like help in transmuting the negative energy, get a Peace Lily plant and put it in the area where most of the negativity arises. Nurture that plant and allow it to change the energy in your space.

Before we begin with the message, the Angels would like to balance your chakras by saying a different chakra prayer; the Archangel Chakra Prayer II. This will help you integrate the information from the message easier. Where there is love, there tends to be fear. So being the strongest you can be on a spiritual level while reading this chapter, will help you recognize any fears that may come up when we are sharing our message.

ARCHANGEL CHAKRA PRAYER II

I call on Archangel Michael to work with me to open and balance my Root Chakra. You help me have courage and integrity. You help me to stay grounded. You help me find my true path for this life. I thank you, Archangel Michael.

I call on Archangel Metatron to work with me to open and balance my Sacral Chakra. You help me have positive thoughts and positive actions. You bring me the energy of joy and remind me to have fun. You help me open up to more abundance in my life. I thank you, Archangel Metatron.

I call on Archangel Uriel to work with me to open and balance my Solar Plexus Chakra. You help me to shine my spiritual *light* as bright as the sun. You help me to understand the power I AM connected to and how to use that power through love. I thank you, Archangel Uriel.

I call on Archangel Raphael to work with me to open and balance my Heart Chakra. You help me remember that I never have to be sick. You remind me that healing *light* is flowing through me every moment. You help open my heart to give and receive a greater love. I AM open to love on all levels. I thank you, Archangel Raphael.

I call on Archangel Tzadkiel to work with me to open and balance my High Heart Chakra. You remind me to have compassion and non-judgment of everyone. I allow each person to walk their own path assisting only when they ask me. You help me follow my heart every day. I thank you, Archangel Tzadkiel.

I call on Archangel Gabriel to work with me to open and balance my Throat Chakra. You help me to find my voice through love and compassion. I speak the truth to myself and to others. You speak through me to help others through inspiring and healing words. I thank you, Archangel Gabriel.

I call on The Holy Spirit to work with me to open and balance my Brow Chakra. You bring me the full power to connect with Spirit. You help me to see the inner *light* in myself and all people. You remind me to see my own beauty, power and healing abilities. I thank You, Holy Spirit.

I call on The Christ Light to work with me to open and balance my Crown Chakra. You help me to radiate pure *light* from Spirit. You help me to know my true self and to see that in others. You remind me to connect to Spirit when I need peace, love and healing. I thank You, Christ Light.

I call on Enoch to work with me to open and balance my Soul Star Chakra. You help me to be a giver of truth. You help me to see more than my human limitations. You remind me to use my intuition and spiritual wisdom every day. You help me be the Divinity that I AM. I thank you, Enoch.

I call on Archangel Chamuel to work with me to open and balance my Zeal Point Chakra. You help me to speak God's words. You remind me that what I speak has power. I use that power through grace, love and *light*. I thank you, Archangel Chamuel.

This subject is about love and how your Angels can help you help yourself. Your Angels are there to do the things that you want them to do, to do your bidding, so to speak. If you are not sending them out to find the highest, greatest love for your life, chances are, in the 4th Dimension, the person is not going to appear on your door step. Prior to the year 2003 that could have happened because we were in the 3rd Dimension, where karma had already determined who would come to you. This meant that you were in relationships that were clearing up some past energy; probably from a past life that you are not even aware of. Because of the karma, we were in situations where we needed to balance lifetimes and learn so when we ended one relationship there was another one just like it waiting for us shortly after the first one ended unless we chose not to go into that cycle again. Since we are in a higher dimension now, we don't need to go through our lessons that way anymore. Some of you have given up on having relationships because of your past relationship history and have convinced yourself that you are doing just fine being alone. But, the Angels came to me and said, *"We have been having difficulty getting the *Lightworkers* to respond with the power and the energy that they have learned how to utilize because their hearts are not open. They have blocks up to prevent love from coming to them. They are very good at giving love to others but when it's time for them to receive, their hearts are blocked or even closed. We understand they put up a block of protection so they don't get hurt like in the past but we need them to understand that they cannot do their highest work on Earth if they are not able to receive love. The more work they do or the higher levels of Spirit they access, the more love they will need to be receiving on Earth to balance the energy."*

A *Lightworker* is anyone on the Earthplane who is striving to connect to themselves more spiritually and one who shares their abilities with others. In order to do that, you share the *light* that flows through you with your friends, your family and the world. That is why they are called *Lightworkers*. You can also be called a *Lightbearer*. *Lightbearers* are people who are constantly flowing *light* to Mother Earth to assist with whatever she needs. To be a *Lightworker* or *Lightbearer* of any assistance to others, you have to have that flow of *light* going in and out. Just think of blood flowing through your veins. If it only flowed in one direction, how long would you be alive? If it only flowed out of your heart but no blood flowed back in to renew it, how long? You need to be renewed. You need to be loved, to be cherished.

If you do not want an intimate love relationship but you still want love in your life, you may ask the Angels for this love to come through a friend or multiple friends. You will probably need more than one friend in order to fulfill this need of receiving love energy. For an intimate relationship, we are talking about a love relationship where your heart is open and exposed and flowing with love going in and love going out. The very first thing to do in order for this love to take place is to forgive. Forgive the past, see the bigger picture. See what happened in your life as a lesson and not through the eyes of ego. If one particular person did something to hurt you, ask to see the situation through the eyes of the Angels. Then you can see that your Soul agreed in spirit that this person would treat you this way so that you would grow to recognize that you deserved more with the expectation that eventually you would honor yourself by getting out of that relationship. Some of us stay too long in relationships because we get comfortable or because we have fear of the unknown; even if we know the current situation we are in is not good for us.

If the relationships that you are still holding emotional ties about happened before 2003, then they really are no longer a part of your life and they are not necessary to hold on to. Everything about your life here on Earth changed when we moved up to the 4th Dimension. They were another person, you were another person. You can literally think of it as a past life that you can remember. The person that you were before 2003 has no bearing on who you are today. This is because when we made the shift, you chose a completely new path for your life and stepped off of the old path. If you feel you are stuck between the old path of ego and karma and the new 4th dimensional path, ask your Angels to be healed or seek out a healer to help you be firmly on the higher path.

Forgiving plays a huge part in allowing the love energy to flow into your life. The Angels recognize this is very hard for us to do. They say that people can go to therapy to release their emotions but it can sometimes take years to get to the core issue. This forgiveness exercise will help you find out the core issue and help you to release it in the easiest, clearest, quickest way. If you are going to therapy, this can be done in tandem with your therapy. This exercise is not one where you to speak to that person face-to-face in order to get the healing. This helps you talk directly to that person's soul. So you avoid the ego that you would be presented with in a face to face situation.

FORGIVENESS EXERCISE

- Write a list of names of people that are currently in your life and from the past.

- As you write each name, take a moment to listen to your thoughts and watch your reactions.

- If you have any reaction other than love or peace with that person, then there are issues left that need to be released from your heart.

- Be honest with yourself during this process.

- Ask your Angels to bring to mind anyone that you may be leaving out.

In order to remove this energy, you would need to forgive those that you perceive have harmed you in some way. All that we experience here shows us more about ourselves. We are here to remember who we are as a piece of God. At this time in our soul development, most of us are just now connecting the dots that we have acquired to see the full picture of our piece. Or said in another way, you may already have all the pieces to your life puzzle on the table and at this time all you have left to do is to figure out where they fit. Some people are in our lives to be the "mean" person so that we can learn our lessons of love and deservedness. These situations are set up ahead of time by contracts between souls before we came into this life.

Here is an example of how this can play out in your life. Think of your life like you are in a play. In this particular play, you are playing the role of the good person and your ex-love is playing the role of the bad person. And they turn out to be excellent at playing their part! At the end of this life when you meet on the other side, like at the end of the play when the curtain goes down, you will laugh and thank this person for being such a great performer at being a bad guy and for sacrificing themselves in your human eyes so that you could learn your lesson. Even in this one life, you may play a different role when you are in other people's plays. We are not always the good person. And we are not always the bad person. We all play many different roles while living here on Earth. When you can see this bigger picture, it is easier to walk away from these situations and forgive those people in your life. You will eventually forgive them; if it is not in this life then it will be when you cross over. Remember, holding a negative feeling in your heart about someone else does nothing to him or her. However, it does make it harder for you to live your life because you will continue to attract situations that will remind you of these people or the issues you had until you release the energy.

Are you ready to release some of this energy? Here is how to do it:

- Get in your Sacred Space…a room where you feel most comfortable that you can speak out loud and will not be disturbed.

- Take three long, slow, deep breaths.

- Spread your arms out to the side, which opens your physical heart and helps to clear any protection you may have over your heart.

- State: "I want to speak with my highest Angels."

- State: "I AM protected." - This makes sure you go only to the Angelic realm.

- You can put your arms down now.

- State: "I want to talk to _____'s Angel." - *Name one person on your list.*

- Immediately that person's Angel is standing in front of you.

- Start talking to that person and telling them what you are holding in your heart. State out loud all the hurt, anger, frustration, etc. that you have felt. Be honest and specific. Just keep talking, things may come out that you were not even aware were still bothering you or that were left unresolved between the two of you.

- When you are done with what the source of the pain was and feel you can forgive, then simply say, "I forgive you, (name)."

- Then state: "I forgive myself for anything that I had to do with these situations and I ask you to forgive me."

- Then tell this person how you would like to proceed. Is this someone from your past that is not in your present or future? Then you can cut the cord between you by stating: "I now cut the cord between us." This causes no physical harm. It releases you from energy that is weighing you down. You will be much lighter once you release the unnecessary attachments from your current life.

- If this is someone that is in your life now that you do not want in your life, you can do the same thing. (Please note, that if there were some lesson that you would be missing by not having this person in your life, another person would enter with the same lesson. Sometimes it is easier going through the lesson with a new person and there is nothing wrong with doing it that way.)

- If this is someone that you want in your life, then use this time to let him or her know the highest way you would like to proceed with your relationship. Would you like to talk with them more or less, see them more or less, be more intimate, be just friends, etc. You are giving them suggestions from the highest level possible on the Earthplane. Because of free-will, they don't have to agree with these suggestions, but their soul will hear you clearly and then can decide how to proceed from their heart and not through ego.

- After you feel you are complete with that person, thank the Angel. This sends the energy back to the person. The Angel's job is to take your forgiveness message to that person and change the message from an egotistical viewpoint into love.

- Keep in mind that it is important for you to speak through ego to release these things because that is where it is stored. As we progress in our spiritual development, we will learn easier ways to not have these things become ego issues and can release it immediately. But for now, this is the easiest way to handle it.

Your side of the energy is changed immediately. For the other person, it will take three days for them to receive the message through their subconscious. If this has to do with someone that you still have in your life, don't expect a change in their energy around you until after the three days have passed.

You may decide to do several persons at a time. If so, you don't need to start at the beginning of the process because you are still connected to your highest Angels. You would start at the point of calling forth their Angel and go from there.

Use this exercise as many times as you need. Sometimes we have so much stuffed down inside that it will come up in layers. Sometimes it is too much to deal with at once. This is a safe way to release your emotions and finally clear out your energy. You can also utilize this exercise each time you feel upset, angry or frustrated with anyone so that it doesn't settle into your emotions or physical body. You can clear up the situation immediately. The hope is that eventually you will be able to say to a person, "I forgive you and I forgive me." And it will be so powerful to bypass any ego and go right to the soul. Until then, you have this exercise.

How do you feel? Do you want to break this tie between you and that other person? Do you want to live with this anger and frustration the rest of your life even though that person is living their life just fine? This is what is holding you back. So, really think about finally releasing it. Take a deep breath, step back and close the door on those areas of your life that are no longer serving you. For some of you, it will be a big step. But it is necessary in order to walk forward in your spiritual growth. The Angels know that you are not reading this message just to feel good, you're reading because you want to know more, you want to connect more to who you are spiritually. You are tired of the way your life is and you want your life to be bigger and better.

Forgiveness of others is the first step. Forgiveness of yourself is even more important. Accept yourself for who you are now. Don't say you will appreciate yourself in six months when you lose 20 pounds. Love yourself right now. You chose this body. Yes, you did. You chose your family, your body type, everything. When you were planning this life, you knew what you had picked out for yourself was perfect and would help you learn the lessons that you needed to learn. Forgive yourself about that if you need to.

Take a moment to walk to a mirror and look yourself in the eyes and say, "I love you!" Keep your eyes open, don't blink or look away. If you blink, it is telling you that you don't really believe what you are saying. It's very difficult, I know. It took me over a week before I could actually do it without blinking.

An important note here: We don't recommend saying anything except this one statement into a mirror because mirrors are spiritual doorways and you can open that doorway by speaking things. And that can get you some unwelcome guests. This will be explained in more detail in a later chapter.

Look directly into your eyes in a mirror and saying, "I love you" is very healing. Your eyes are the windows to your soul. You are speaking directly to the core of who you are at that moment. When you say this, you are not saying you're going to love yourself in six months, or a year, or when you get a better job, or when someone loves you, or anything else. You are committing to love yourself now. In this time of our life on Earth, everything is about now. And now is the time to change your life.

Accept that you are worthy of love and know that God loves

you. He loves you no matter what you have done, no matter what your thoughts have been or the actions you have taken. No matter who you hurt, it doesn't matter. God loves you exactly as you are today. The hardest part for us is understanding that we are worthy of love even though we have a past filled with negativity and egotistical choices.

An Angel just popped in and is telling you to take a deep breath and breathe out. Is it hard to hear that you are worthy of God's love now, right now as you sit there reading this book? Breathe in deep; feeling His love all around you. His love is always all around you. You just may not have noticed it before.

In the 4th Dimension, now that we are not learning our lessons through karma, it makes sense to want the highest and best relationship we can have. In your thoughts do you still want someone to complete you? In a football movie, I loved it when Tom Cruise said, "You complete me." It was such a beautiful statement so perfect for the 3rd Dimension; yet so backwards from where we stand now. What 4th dimensional people who feel they are worthy are seeking is the highest and greatest love for their life. That would mean you are a complete, spiritual human being and the other person is a complete, spiritual human being. You are not asking someone to come fix you because you are already doing that for yourself or have already done that. And you are not looking for someone that you need to fix or change. You want them to be responsible for themselves. You are looking for that whole person who will make your heart sing, not make it heavy by working hard. That is the best description of a 4th dimensional person seeking a love relationship.

The way that you spiritually call forth this wonderful, full spiritual human being who is the greatest match for you is to have already balanced your chakras with a chakra prayer of intention. Then you put your shoulders back. This opens your chest area, allowing your heart to be more open and exposed. Immediately what happens is a green *light* from your Heart Chakra spiritually comes out of your heart in a beam. According to how open your heart is, the beam will shine through. If your heart is open only a little bit because you have it tied up to the past, hold unforgiveness in your heart or are controlled by your ego, then the beam will be like a penlight or a little flicker of *light*. If it's opened a lot more, it will be like a flashlight, which will be easier for another person's soul to see and recognize as a match for them. The best opening to receive the highest, greatest love is to be like a lighthouse, which shines through the thickest fog, strong and powerful. The way to be a lighthouse is to have worked through all forgiveness issues and keep doing so each time a new situation comes up.

With your chakras open and your shoulders back and with your intentions strong that you want the greatest, highest love in your life now, then this *light* that is shining from your heart will go out into the Universe searching until it finds your match. Every day, everywhere you go, this *light* beam goes from your aura into the world. As you meet people, your *light* will recognize other people's *light* and you will see and fell spiritually who is the right match for you.

Let's say that you are somewhat protected and you have this little flashlight of a *light* coming out of your heart, yet you are asking for the highest and greatest love. The most relationship that you are going to receive will be equal to the *light* that you are sending out. You will have someone come into your life that is also protecting their heart. You will meet someone that will be the same resonation that you are sending out. Therefore, to pull forth the highest, greatest love into your life, you need the lighthouse kind of *light* beaming from your heart to find someone who is beaming out a lighthouse *light* from their heart. That's why the Angels are always saying through my teachings, "Your past is not your future." If you change the brightness of the *light* that is in your heart by releasing lower, negative energy, you can receive a different type of person than the past. This is only possible since we moved to the 4th dimension because the karmic ties were severed. If we had not moved into a higher dimension, you would be reading an entirely different chapter of how to accept less than the best because even though you are clearing up the past there would be nothing you could do about who karma brought to you. Knowing that living on Earth at this time is a blessing to your soul and that you have more control over your own experience, I am sure you want to be as strong and powerful a *light* as possible.

When this person comes to you, you will know it. You will feel it in your heart. Your heart may skip a beat. Your heart may flutter. Your heart may sing with joy. You will know. If someone comes to you and you are not feeling it and you find yourself trying to logically tell if this is the one, then they are definitely not the one.

Answer this question: What makes your heart leap for joy? This isn't an answer the Angels are going to give you. Ask yourself: What is it that makes me happy? The Angels are saying whatever your answer is, do more of it. Someone in Spirit is laughing and saying, "And if it's chocolate, then just bless it before you eat it." So what is it? What makes your heart leap for joy?

We want to show you and have you feel the feeling of love. The tingling feeling that you get when you meet someone and you know that person is the one. When you are in that zone and are spiritually open and connected, you are going to be a powerful force for good across this Earth and across the Universe. Your thoughts will become things. You will have higher thoughts to create higher energy. You won't even think, "I need to think the right thing." You will already be in that zone. That is why it is important to have the highest, greatest love in your life. I have seen this happen. I have channeled this for people in their private Soul Sessions. The Angels have shared with them exactly how to do this and they have these higher relationships walking into their lives. And even though they asked for it, for some it is unbelievable to them that they actually have a different kind of person loving them than from the past. It's wonderful!

I do need to explain something. This doesn't mean that the person that is coming to you is going to have no issues or that you will have no issues within the relationship. You will always be learning lessons while you are on the Earthplane. And the easiest way we learn lessons is through our loved ones. Very rarely will you meet a person that you will not teach to or learn from. Every soul does that. They either teach or they learn or do both with every other soul that they meet. However, the difference here in the 4th dimension is that you can learn the lessons from someone that loves you in an easier way because you are less likely to judge each other; you are looking at each other with more compassion and allowing each other to walk your own paths. In our ego-type relationships from the 3rd Dimension that had the karma, we met people, we loved them, and then we wanted to change them. In the beginning of the relationship we might have said, "I'll just fix that personality trait I don't like about them later." That is not what we are to do now. We are supposed to work on ourselves and raise our own *light* and then naturally, because we are close to our partner, they will get the benefit of the *light* that we are exuding. If they are doing the same thing, then we will get the benefit of the *light* that they are exuding. It's a win-win situation. We are not saying that this will be a Disney World vacation 365 days a year, but we are saying that you will be happier, more joyful and you will experience a love like you have never experienced in any lifetime while learning your love lessons.

Whether you recognize it or not, you have been working all of your lives and all of this life up to this moment to be able to hear this and to accept this energy. You are ready to hear that it is okay to ask for something like this because you do deserve it. *Lightworkers* are really good at getting out and saying "I don't really need a relationship. I can take care of myself." If this describes you stop and think about this for a moment. You are not going to be able to sustain yourself very well as you ascend unless

◄ YOUR DIVINE LIFE

you have love surrounding you in your life. The higher you go the more love in your Earthplane life you are going to need or it will get increasingly harder to stay in balance.

Like we said before, whether it is an intimate relationship or whether you decide to get the love through friends, make the distinction to the Angels and they will bring forth whatever it is that you are seeking.

What I am being told right now is that there are two Archangels that want to speak directly to you about love. During their message, if you need a healing, make your intentions strong so that it will be complete and perfect. Also, breathe deep during the message. It is important to know that this is coming from a higher source and it is flowing through me directly to your heart.

"Greetings! We are Raphael and Uriel. We are here to straighten out these issues from your past and give you strength and peace for your future. You have lived many lives in dark sorrow in order to learn the lessons to remove yourselves from ego. These lessons are behind you and because of the collective decision to move to the higher dimension of energy, the opportunity for a different kind of love is now available to you. We ask that you breathe through any fear that you have regarding this subject of love. This higher, greater love cannot enter your life if you are resistant. We are offering you a gift, a blessing. There is no need

to fear. Understand you always have a choice. If what we bring to you is not acceptable, or you change your mind you may walk away at any time. All we are asking is for you to open your heart and allow us to show you what you can have.

This new level of love will change you in many ways, ways that are unknown to you right now. You will grow and as you grow, you will bless many others even through your daily walk of life. You will bless the Earth. You will bless the Heavens. We are asking for your permission to bring this to you for we cannot without your intention. This is not a karmic relationship. We understand what you are seeking and we hear the points that you are making about what you do not want. And if you trust us then we will bring you that which is equal to your heart's *light*. There is a fire of passion burning within you that has barely been ignited in this life. As you relax and open up to love, your fire will burn stronger and brighter. We trust that you will be very pleased with the outcome of this adventure.

You know us as we know you. Trust us as we trust you. Love yourself as we love you. You deserve the peace, the love and the wonderful life that you have always wanted.

We are going now but we are never far. We speak to you through your heart. Just look for us there and we will answer your questions. Be peace. And be love."

Take a deep breath. Allow that energy to flow through you. Breathe out. Thank you, Archangels!

Now, if you would like some specific help in this area of love from your Angels, go get a piece of paper. I am going to give you some questions to ask your Angels. As always when you are consciously connecting to Spirit, you should state a prayer. You can say your own or say this one:

"I thank You, Lord for Your love and Your *light* as I call forth the highest Angels to bring information that is clear, helpful and useful for my life today. I thank You for Your protection as I do so. I thank You, that I AM that clear and pure channel of love and *light*. Amen."

Remember as you read each question out loud, you just write down the very first answer that comes to mind. Don't stop to analyze anything. Just write until there are no more words or feelings to express. And then move on to the next question continuing until you are done.

~ Angels, what do I need to release to get the highest and greatest joy and love to walk into my life?

~ Angels, who do I need to forgive to bring this highest and greatest joy into my life?

~Angels, what more do I need to do to bring this highest and greatest joy and love into my life?

Having received that information you can follow up with a forgiveness exercise or whatever else the Angels suggested in their answers to help you be in the highest energy before you go to the next part.

Now you are going to ask to have this wonderful person come into your life. Take a deep breath in and place your arms out to your sides. This opens up your heart. Stand or sit in the form of a cross with both feet flat on the floor. (Doing the breathing the way it is described here is very important.)

Take a deep breath in. Breathe out.

"I thank You, Lord that I now have the highest and greatest love in my life now."

Take a deep breath in. Breathe out.

"I thank You that I am committed to being the highest, greatest love for the person that You bring to me."

Take a deep breath in. Breathe out.

"Show me what, if anything, I need to do to bring this person into my life."

Take a deep breath in and breathe out.

"I thank You that I now see the signs clearly of who this person is that is the highest, greatest love for me now."

Take a deep breath in and breathe out.

"I thank You."

Bring your hands in front of your heart in prayer form and breathe in, believing you will receive what you have asked.

Here are some affirmations to assist in bringing the higher and greater love you deserve into your life.

"I AM love."

"I deserve to receive love."

"I AM open to giving and receiving love in a greater way every day."

"I AM a powerful force for good."

"I AM now ready for the highest and greatest love to walk into my life."

"I AM in the perfect relationship."

"I AM pure *light* and pure love."

"I AM blessed in my love relationship and I AM a blessing to my love."

"I AM aware of God's love for me."

CATE'S STORY OF LETTING GO

I ended a nine year relationship, with a man I thought was my soul mate. Although there were many indicators of trouble during the two years leading up to the break up, I kept trying to fix things, as I thought the spiritual gifts of the connection were worth cleaning up the real life stuff. But the big shift to the 4th Dimension caused us to be sent in different directions.

This man, who I had loved, was still in my heart. For over a year, I practiced release methods, affirmations, psychological insights and utilized various healers to help me sever the ties to him. I just couldn't get him out of my head.

When I called Christina for a Soul Session, she and the Angels asked that I do this simple visualization when I got off of the phone:

"Imagine him as an Eagle and he is flying high, and you are holding on to his legs.... when you are ready, let go and he will fly away."

I thought - SIMPLE! I was shocked when after holding my arms up in the air for 15 minutes; I still couldn't let him go!!! It was me who was still holding onto him. All that time I thought it was him who was holding onto me. I cried and cried but finally was able to let him go. My insight afterward was that I had let him go on a lot of levels.

In a past life Christina had explained he had been my child - a child I couldn't protect or save and what I was feeling was that I did not want to risk losing my child again. I had to really embrace that he was no longer my child to protect and save and acknowledge he was God's child. And I needed to absolve myself of that guilt and grief. I had to let go! I was able to see our relationship from a much more loving and detached viewpoint after this exercise and was able to move on.

ASCENSION SYMPTOMS

SO many of you are going through physical symptoms and emotional symptoms that make it seem like you are not progressing. It may even seem like you are going backwards on your spiritual journey. For most of you, it is not that you are going backwards; it is actually that you are finally able and ready to purge lower energy from your body so that you can ascend into the next dimension. The Angels explained that with each move up to a new dimension there is a catalyst that starts the process. For the jump from the 1st to 2nd dimension it was the biblical flood. For the jump from the 2nd to the 3rd dimension, it was Jesus becoming Jesus Christ, forgiving on the cross. And for the 3rd to the 4th dimension it was a collective soul consciousness choice to remain on Earth and remember who we are. To move from one dimension to another, there need to be 144,000 souls resonating at a certain vibration equal to that dimension all at the same time in order to catapult the rest of the Earthplane into that dimension. (An interesting side note, it took one man, Jesus Christ to do this on His own. For all the other dimensional shifts it has taken and will take 144,000 souls to make it happen.)

Once these fore-runners (*Lightworkers* and *Lightbearers*) do this and can maintain that energy they will be walking between the two dimensions and then everyone else on the Earthplane will start to go through these symptoms. So the fore-runners go through them first while they are anchoring the higher energy. Right now, you may be going through these ascension symptoms and there will be others around you that are not because they are not walking a conscious spiritual path. That is appropriate because you chose yourself to be one of the first ones to walk over into the new dimension. As a soul, you knew it wouldn't be easy to be in the first wave; however you were willing to walk into the unknown. And because of that you will be helping those behind you have it easier when they go through it at a later time.

No two souls will ever go through the same symptoms, in the same order for the same amount of time. The purging process has to do with what experiences each soul has gone through in its many Earth lifetimes and where it is going next. Do not compare your process with someone else. One way is not better than another. Please be supportive to each other because ascension is not easy on the physical or emotional body and everyone will need some support.

ASCENSION SYMPTOMS

When you are going through these symptoms try to remember that this is an answer to your prayer, conscious or otherwise, that you want to ascend. Don't let these symptoms push you into fear. It shows you are resonating more *light* in your body. It is saying, "You have done the work and now you are ready to ascend."

When you are ascending into a higher physical dimension on Earth, you are literally changing the cells in your body. You are moving and opening them so that more *light* can flow through them than before. You are replacing the cells that are damaged; these are the cells that cannot hold a higher vibration. These damaged cells are being replaced with new *lighter* cells. Just imagine that you are growing a new body that is going to be much *lighter* and less dense and then you can understand how it might hurt sometimes during the process of change. Think of it as growing pains. When you are going through this process try to remember it is not punishment; it is a blessing based on how wonderful a job you are doing in your spiritual walk.

What is a physical symptom of the ascension? What emotions might come up during this period? Some of the symptoms of ascension are:

- Memory loss or problems retaining information

- Changes in family situations

- Changes in friends, jobs, residences

- Sleeping problems; waking between 2:00am and 4:00am

- Times of deep sleep, tiredness, extreme fatigue

- Night sweats

- Ringing in the ears

- Heart palpitations

- Body vibrations

- Muscle cramps in legs and shoulders

- Neck pain

- Skin rashes

- Aches and pains in the body for no reason

- Clumsiness, Dizziness

- Cravings for different foods

- Disorientation

- Changes in your prayer or meditation experiences

- Panic or depression

- Weeping, feelings of loss

- Feelings of wanting to go "home"

These are only some of the symptoms but you get the idea. We would like you to be observant of your body. Make sure that you check first to see if there is a physical reason as to why you are having that particular issue. When you find out that you are healthy and there is no reason for it, you know it is an ascension symptom. There is a reason we have doctors here on Earth. Be smart and use them when necessary. Another way to confirm if you are ascending is to ask your Angels.

There are three ways you can go through the Ascension. One is to do nothing. You go through at the pace your soul has already decided. It will vary with each person as no two persons are exactly at the same level. The second is to ask your Angels to slow down the process so that it is not disruptive to your daily life; meaning you will only notice the slight physical or emotional symptoms. It will take you longer to go through the ascension but that may be appropriate with the responsibilities you have in your life. The third way is to have your Angels speed it up and get it over with. We only recommend this if you are feeling strong and otherwise healthy and have sufficient time to rest. Most of the time, you can do this over a long weekend where you can just rest at home. Be sure to be ready for the consequences. I always do it the sped up way but I work from home. Sometimes it gets pretty uncomfortable but at least I know it will be over soon.

You won't go through all of the symptoms at the same time, which is a blessing, so when you are done with one issue don't be surprised when a short time later another issue (or two or three) shows up. Once you are complete in that particular part of the ascension process, the symptoms that apply will cease to occur.

Sometimes it will be difficult to remember that you asked for this. You always have a choice about how fast you want to go through your ascension. If you change your mind and decide a different way tomorrow, that is fine. You always have a choice. More than ever before, you are in control of your soul's development.

A KEY FOR YOUR HEART

A CHANNELED MESSAGE FROM ENOCH

"**WE** wish to give you something to assist you with leaving fear behind. Sit up straight with your shoulders back. Take deep, slow breaths. Place your concentration on your heart. Look with your inner eye at your heart. Place your hand out in front of you. See or feel your Angel in front of you. Continue to breathe deep. Your Angel, that higher part of your Soul that serves only you, is handing you a key. You are able to receive this key now because of all of the work that you have done in your Soul's development. Close your hand over the key and take the key to your heart. As you breathe, your heart expands like an accordion, allowing *light* to flow in and out. You have a physical heart and you have a Heart Chakra residing a few inches out from your heart. In between the two, there is a space. In that space, there is a box. This box has been locked for all of your time on Earth. Place the key in the lock and feel the flood of energy of love and *light* as you turn the key to open this area once and forever. Feel love coursing through your body at a faster and higher rate than ever before. The energy that you feel is love, *light*, knowledge and wisdom. These are all spiritual blessings you have access to now at a higher level than ever before. This has been hard earned and we honor you for being ready to unlock this box. Continue to breathe and feel your heart swell, comfortably. Now visualize out of your heart, through your Heart Chakra is a river. This river of *light* is flowing out of your heart and into the depths of Mother Earth. This river of *light* is flowing out of you to each and every Soul that resides in this Universe. This energy is flowing through you and out through this opening that you now have access to. Continue to breathe. Now see diamonds flow out of this river of *light*. The diamonds flow freely from the Heavens through the dimensions down through you and this heart opening that you have unlocked. These diamonds are thoughts, pure and innocent, loving and filled with *light* that will now be flowing through you to others. You will be saying things that you have never said before. With love and pure intent you will be teaching from higher levels. These are the things that you have earned. This is our gift to you for a job well done. We wish to honor you for all that you have done, suffered and sacrificed in this time of illusion that you are separate. We know that it is hard to understand the concept of separateness and that it is an illusion for it seems so real to you. We honor that you are trying to understand these concepts without concrete evidence for your *logical minds. The road has been long, dark and difficult but you have always had the power, you have always had access to the love and you always knew how to get home. Now you will know these things more consciously. As you look to your future remember what you are capable of, remember that you are the balance that people will turn to and seek out in times of negative situations. The more balanced and strong and powerful you are in the *light* the more you will be able to help. And these people you will help will have a domino effect to help others. It is important for you to stay strong in the midst of chaos or tragedy and know that all is in divine order. We (Enoch) don't speak often but we are always watching over you. We will be assisting you more during the years to come as you continue to ascend to become a brighter spark of *light*. We love you."*

LIVING WELL

~ To participate in the exercise within this chapter, we recommend having a small snack of your choice ready to eat. ~

THE Angels have shared with me information on how to have a healthy spiritual human life. This includes information on how to have a clearer spiritual connection daily, how to love yourself more, how to lose weight or maintain a healthy weight. It has been a very interesting journey learning this and surprisingly very easy.

To start, I recommend that you say a prayer. (We recommend you always say a prayer before you open up any spiritual connection to aid in your discernment, protection and so that you are a clear channel to reach the highest levels of Spirit possible.) Here is a prayer that I say:

"I thank You, Lord for Your love and Your *light* as I call forth the highest Angels to bring information that is clear, helpful and useful for today. I thank You for Your protection as I do so and I thank You that I am that clear and pure channel of love and *light*. Amen."

For this exercise, I would like for you to have a snack in front of you. It can be anything…chocolate, ice cream, candy, cake, anything you like. Go ahead and take a bite of your snack. While you are chewing your snack, notice how it tastes. Finish your bite and set the snack aside. That's all we are going to do with that right now. We'll come back to it later.

The Angels have said that the very first thing to do when you wake up in the morning is to spend a few minutes thanking Spirit for having another day on Earth to learn and to share with others what you have already learned. This is best before your feet touch the floor. The way I do that is to spread my arms apart, opening up my breast bone, which opens up my heart and expressing to the Universe my thankfulness. Some days, I really don't feel like it, but because I start out the day doing it anyway, I end up having a much better day than if I had chosen not to do it. Trust me and try it. You will see a difference in your day if you do this. When you are in that twilight stage and spending that extra snooze time instead of sleeping go ahead and connect to the Universe, you will have a much stronger spiritual connection throughout the day. That is really the best time for you to open up to the Universe.

Most people brush their teeth in the morning or take a sip of water to rinse out their mouth. The Angels told me to drink a whole glass of water as soon as I get up. You might be saying, "Yuck!" like I did when they told me. Drinking water helps your body regulate itself every day. It will also help you to get your daily requirement of water if you start after you wake up and you will also notice that you will feel lighter throughout the day.

The Angels have shared that many of us have health / weight issues because we are emotionally rejecting our bodies. In Spirit, when we were preparing to come into our Earthplane experience, we picked these particular bodies. No one tricked us. It's the truth. I know it may be hard to believe because some of us think we never would have chosen this body or these weight issues. You chose your family, you chose the issues you were going to learn, you chose your path, your skin color, your eyes, what country you were going to be born in, your religion, everything. Our bodies are our representation of God; this is our temple to God. We should honor it as such. Knowing this, I was asking an Angel, "How do I lose weight because I really don't like how I look right now?" And the Angel reminded me of what they shared earlier saying, "Look in the mirror, eyeball to eyeball at yourself and say, 'I love you' without blinking." I didn't believe those words when I said them and my body rejected the feeling too. The Angels know that when you open your eyes and look eye to eye with someone, you see into their soul. So, in the mirror, you are telling your soul that you love your physical-ness; you love your whole being's presence on the Earthplane. I suggest that you try this powerful exercise. This mirror exercise will jumpstart your connection to releasing your fears, your anger, anything that you feel about your body. It will show you how you really feel about yourself. This will help put it back on the right track. Once you feel better about your body, then you will be able to release the weight easier. Or if you don't want to lose weight, that's fine, you can stop from gaining any weight. Either way say "I love you" to yourself at least once a day, no matter what. (*We do not recommend saying anything else in front of the mirror. Mirrors are spiritual windows and your words can be powerful. We will explain more about this in the story following this chapter.*)

The Angels say that when you are taking a shower, thank your body. When you are washing your hands, thank your hands for letting you be able to reach things, for being able to hold things. Thank your arms for supporting you and being able to lift things. Thank your legs for being strong enough to walk and for supporting your entire body. Thank your chest for giving you the breath of life that you need. And thank your feet for staying on the easy path and reminding yourself that you want to be on the easiest path of life. Remember, to thank God for all of your body parts whenever you are washing them. Even thank God for the parts of you that seem to be rejecting you right now. For example, if you have an issue with your thyroid, when you are washing your throat or just rubbing it, state that your thyroid is in perfect condition and thank it for working perfectly. If you have been told you have a cancer in your body, rub that part of your body and lovingly bless it for being perfect and for regaining its balance and returning to normal.

Our brain is extremely powerful and we are capable of accomplishing so much just due to our thoughts. Your body ultimately wants to be in balance and when you are overweight, you are not in balance. If you start working with your brain telling it what you want it to do, it will respond to you and start doing it. Ultimately, your brain is the one that wants everything to be perfect.

Now about exercising. You knew we were going to talk about this eventually! I don't exercise a lot and it seemed that whenever I did, I end up hurting myself or working out too hard. I used to work out 150% rather than gradually increasing. In this case, the Angels told me that it is not necessary for you to go out and exercise five to six times per week. What the Angels would like people to do is to walk more. You can add this into your daily routine. Just park at the end of the parking lot, as long as it is safe, and walk into the store rather than getting a front parking space. You can also take the stairs instead of the elevator. You can walk around the mall once before you start shopping. You can walk your shopping cart back into the grocery store. You can do many things each day to walk more.

For myself, I go to a gym and walk on a treadmill since I cannot run or jog because of my jaw surgery. After the surgery, I asked the Angels what I was going to do and they said, "Just walk." That's all. And with doing what the Angels told me about walking one hour two to three times a week for two months, doing the blessing of the food and consciously eating, I lost twenty-three pounds.

Most of the exercise instructors you see on TV say to exercise five or six days per week. If you can do that, great! Then you are going to lose weight even faster. I wasn't ready for that. Anything you do that is more, then you will lose more and definitely be burning more calories. But don't push yourself. Just do what you can and gradually add to that.

Another aspect of the weight issues are medical related. A lot of us have thyroid issues or different medical issues which slow our metabolism down. We recommend seeing your doctor regularly. You may find out you have something interfering with your metabolism. Get a physical which would include having your blood pressure checked. With the multi-dimensional healings that are available in this energy, we are working in tandem with the doctors. Every healing is different. Sometimes people need medicine. We recommend confirming your healing with a doctor and following your doctor's advice on how and when to wean off of any medications you are taking. This is important to know now because with these Angelic tools for raising the vibration of your body, you may see healing results immediately.

The prayer that the Angels are going to give you shortly will also help with your medications. Medicines are made for thousands of people and yet you are just one person for one particular issue and you are taking that medicine, so it may be too much or not enough for you. There may be side-effects or it may not even be enough for what you should have. You can use this prayer to help raise or lower the vibration so that the medication is exactly what you need. You can use this prayer with your vitamins, herbs or whatever you are taking. Each time you get a new bottle of medicine, hold the bottle in your hands in front of your heart and pray the prayer we will share with you. When you get a new bottle of medication, do the prayer again. Also, another key is to write the word "Love" directly on the bottle. This also puts a higher vibration into the medicine. Whenever you pick up the bottle, your thoughts will be directed toward love instead of frustration that you are taking a pill. Whatever direction our thoughts go in is where the energy is directed. Do you think you will heal faster through thinking about love or by being frustrated about your physical sickness or disease? The answer is, you heal through love.

We are all so unique with what our bodies need and the type of systems we have, whether it is a sluggish or fast metabolism, and yet we are taking pills made for a set group of millions of people. No, the Angels are not suggesting you get off your medication. Medications serve a purpose. We will be showing you how to gain control of your life and how to get the most out of your medication. This will help you move towards healing so you eventually won't need any medication. Won't that be a wonderful day?! The Angels are suggesting that you hand-hold with Spirit and you call forth your healing of these particular things and let them heal you. You can ask for anything through your Angels. The key is believing you can receive a healing and that you deserve it.

Right now we would like you to take another bite of your snack.

◄ YOUR DIVINE LIFE

Pay attention to how it tastes. After you are done, put the snack down and continue reading.

Now the Angels would like to talk about the way you are eating food. This is not a diet. This is a way to eat everything by changing the vibration of the food or snack through a prayer of blessing. You will not be limited on the types of food that you can eat. In fact, the Angels have shared with me that it is not in your best interest to do so. Instead, you should be eating from all of the food groups and limiting how much you eat of each one so that you are getting a variety of foods and nutrients. There are three things that can cause weight and disease issues where food is concerned. One is the vibration of the food. Second are the emotional issues of whoever is eating the food. Third, there can be an issue because of the inherited body type. Whether you want to lose weight, maintain a certain weight or just be healthy, these tips will help you.

This may be obvious but I am told to point it out anyway. We eat too much. We have big plates and big bowls which allow us to eat a lot of food. You may not know what the correct portion size is for your body. If you have any doubts, go to the store, buy a small package of the dinner sized plates with dividers and then see what sized portions your body needs. These plates have a large place for the meat, a smaller place for the potatoes and a smaller place for the vegetables. The Angels said that we are used to eating unconsciously or better said, we are not consciously eat-

LIVING WELL

ing. We are just sticking the food in our mouths and swallowing during dinner time. We are not really thinking about the portion sizes or how this food is blessing us.

A couple of years ago I went from eating salads in a small bowl to a large salad bowl then to a large spaghetti bowl during dinner. I justified it by telling myself, "It's just a salad and salads are healthy." But then I started gaining weight that I was later unsuccessful at losing. I have never dieted so I tried to lose the weight through exercising. That didn't work and then the Angels gave me this priceless tip about the portion size of my food.

Please note: If you try this, the Angels do not want you to go from the portion size you are eating now down to the size of the dividers in the plates they mentioned if it is drastic. Make the changes gradually. This is not something meant to make you hungry; this is something that is meant to be a way of life. You can gradually decrease the amount of food you eat.

The other thing is that I love Diet Coke. The Angels have told me that this isn't the greatest drink for me to be drinking. But, I told them, "I don't drink alcohol. I don't smoke. I don't do drugs. I don't do any of those things but I like my Diet Coke. Can I keep drinking my Diet Coke?" So the Angels made me a deal. Here it is: If you like soda or coffee, for every soda or coffee you drink, you drink the same amount of water. You can still drink what you love, but this will help your body regulate and flush out the effects of what you are drinking. Your body needs pure water. I used to think that water was in Diet

Coke so that counted as one of my daily glasses of water but that isn't so. Your body doesn't change the water that is in the Diet Coke into the water that it needs. So you do need to be drinking water to allow your body to function at its highest level. Obviously, if you are drinking regular Coke, sodas or drinks with calories, then you would need to cut back on those drinks to lose weight and still drink an even exchange of water. Most people focus on the food that they eat and don't even think that their drinks could be causing a weight issue.

I also used to like a lot of salt on my food. The Angels had me change from using iodized salt to sea salt. You can use less sea salt and still get the same taste. And after a while, they told me to stop adding it when I was cooking. Then they said that I should stop adding it on my food after it was cooked because in the majority of our canned or processed foods, there is already salt added. I then asked what I could do to help with the taste and they said I could add pepper. I've now been adding pepper to my foods which helps me with the taste. Lately, I have been very creative with adding basil on sandwiches and other spices when I am cooking and haven't even missed the salt.

The Angels said that I can use butter but I have to use less of it to lose weight. It doesn't have to be drastic, just less. Same goes for the salad dressing. I didn't recognize at the time how much I was pouring on my salads. They said that if you are holding the bottle upside down for four seconds; then only hold it upside down for two seconds. And if you put the salad dressing on the side, you can control the amount you use even more. Even better is just dipping your fork in the dressing that you have on the side and then picking up your salad. I made all of these changes without affecting the taste of my food. I didn't really notice the differences but I recognized I was eating less and I was enjoying my food more. It was like I was participating more in the preparation of my food and I was making more conscious choices.

That's what the prayer does for you. It's kind of sneaky. When you say this prayer of blessing for your food, you are essentially thanking the Universe for changing the vibration of the food in front of you to be exactly what you need. And what your body doesn't need, you pray it is easily released from your body. What this does behind the scenes is start a dialogue with your brain to say, "Ok, we want to lose weight (or maintain weight) so let's start making better choices about what we're eating." I didn't realize that at first. If you are stating the prayer three to five times per day over meals and snacks, you are really going to hook into this energy and release these issues about how you eat quickly.

The Angels also told me snacking is important. Every two hours, go ahead and snack on a yogurt, fruit or something light yet satisfying. All those little snack packs they have at the store for convenience are great. Fresh fruit would be better but if you can't have that, buy the can fruit. If you do, then you can buy the cans with the light syrup. Every little change you make will help you. Snacking every two hours is great so that when it comes time for you to eat dinner you are not as hungry. That way you won't eat as much or even put as much on your plate. Remember with the blessing you can have a snack later that night, too.

The energy for working toward losing weight is concentrated within our physical-ness, specifically our Sacral Chakra. It is appropriate that when you are working on losing weight and becoming more balanced in that area, that you would call on Archangel Metatron. Archangel Metatron has shared with me that he will help anyone who asks him. It also helps to do the Chakra prayers and affirmations because they always state wonderful things about your body which helps you to learn to love yourself and your body.

One of the things that we haven't touched on is about worry and guilt. If you eat something and you feel guilty about it, you have immediately lowered the vibration of that food and it becomes denser within your body and can be converted into fat. If you are going to eat something, choose to eat it, but never feel guilty about it. *This is a really good lesson for all of your life. Whatever you do in life, choose to do it but don't feel guilty about it. Make conscious choices.* If you ever find yourself feeling guilty about eating something, I would recommend you stop eating it until you can get in a better frame of mind. Then when you are, bless it, choose to eat it and feel really happy about what you are doing. Really enjoy it!

That was the main area that I was having an issue with other than having the body that was passed down to me through my family line that I chose for this life. I felt guilty about eating certain things and if I left food on my plate. I was used to not knowing if I would have food for the next meal so I learned very early to eat everything I could that was in front of me. I am still a work in progress because to this day, I have been unsuccessful with not finishing everything on my plate. (I heard so many times growing up about all the starving children in Africa and how grateful they would be to have the food that was on my plate.) So the Angels suggestion of not putting as much on my plate worked very well for me because then I could finish the plate and not feel guilty.

When the Angels told me it was good to eat chocolate, I was so excited! Chocolate is fantastic for making us feel better. Scientists have proven it. The Angels told me we just have to change our thoughts about it. I was thinking negative thoughts while I would eat the chocolate and that was not for my highest good. If you want to eat chocolate, eat it. Just don't feel guilty about it. Isn't that amazing!? That is such a blessing because everyone likes chocolate!

When you eat your food, it is best to be sitting down. With the invention of the TV, a lot of us have moved from sitting with our families at the dining room table to eating in front of the TV. This makes it difficult to appreciate the food and consciously eat. It would be best to eat without distractions. Perhaps put on some soft music. After you say the prayer, take a bite of food and taste it. Don't just chew a few times and swallow it. Taste it. Enjoy it. Appreciate the act of giving your body life. I know it may not be a fine wine but treat each bite as though it is very precious. You will be amazed at how much you enjoy your food when you consciously eat!

Following is the prayer that the Angels have given me to share with you can be used to aid in losing weight, maintaining weight, blessing our food, medications and supplements.

"I thank You, Lord that this food is exactly the vibration and energy that I need for cellular regeneration and spiritual development. I thank You that anything more than my body needs right now and would normally be converted into fat is immediately released. I thank You that I continue to lose weight in a healthy way to _____ pounds. My body will meet my maintenance weight of _____ pounds easily and quickly. Amen."

For bottles of medications, vitamins, supplements:

"I thank You, Lord that this medication is exactly the vibration and energy that I need for cellular regeneration and perfect health. I thank You that anything more than my body needs right now is immediately released from my system. If I need more medication than this provides I ask that You increase it. I am perfectly healthy today!"

You can also say this prayer over the individual pills as you have a headache or some special onetime situation. If you have already written the word "Love" on the bottle, this can be your reminder that you know you have blessed the medication.

Let me also mention that it was difficult for me to lose weight when I prayed to lose 25 pounds. I didn't lose it as quickly because I really didn't believe that it could happen. So I decided to go back, at the Angels' urging, and say the prayer in five or ten pound increments. Any prayer that you state, you truly need to believe that you can do it because you are the one sending out the energy to the Universe stating that this is going to be done. If it is believable to you and you are really happy and excited about it, then it's going to manifest really quick. But if you say the prayer not believing it can really happen, it won't happen. Make it believable to yourself and do it in increments knowing that when you lose the first five or ten pounds then you'll start praying to lose another five or ten. This is a healthy way to do this.

Now let's get back to your snack. Go ahead and say the prayer again with the snack in your hand. Always take deep breaths before and after stating your prayers and remember to smile! This is something you should be excited about. After all, you are changing the vibration of what you want for your life. The Angels would like you now to take a bite of your snack. They want you to chew it consciously, tasting it, enjoying it, no guilt, no worries. You have just changed the vibration of that snack to be perfect for your body. How does it taste? Does it taste any different than it did for the first bite? For me, the taste gets richer and you can taste the different aspects of it. Now take another bite and really just enjoy it! You deserve to reward yourself!

I invite you to use these tools and to use the blessing. Weigh yourself no more than once a week. Also weigh yourself at the same time of day, preferably in the morning. If I can do it, you can do it.

Just try these Angel tools for a couple of weeks and see what it does for you. I believe you can have the body that you want!

MY STORY OF A SPIRITUAL WINDOW

MY children grew up thinking we lived a super-natural life. When we would come home together before we walked in our front door, we would practice our intuitive skills by all saying how many messages were on the answering machine. Or who was on the answering machine. Or how many emails someone received since the last time they checked. It was a fun way to teach them to integrate their abilities into their daily life. As they got older the lessons changed to asking "Is it safe to go out tonight with my friends to go dancing?" And things like that. As I learned something I would often speak about it in front of them, always being truthful even when I did something that didn't turn out the way I expected. I figured they could learn from my spiritual mis-steps.

This particular day I noticed that our home was spiritually more active but not with Angels. I could feel a presence that wasn't supposed to be there. I work with the realm of the Angels (and above) so I don't normally deal with the people who are crossed over. They are in different dimensions. I have been very clear spiritually that I don't want my home to be a place that they visit. So I was surprised to feel someone from that realm there. I didn't take the time to ask who they were or what they wanted, I just dismissed it thinking they would go away. Then disruptive things started happening. Open doors shut. The feeling of wind when there was no open window. Things started getting louder and escalated to the point of a five pound bag of potatoes flying off the top of the microwave. Luckily no one was in the kitchen at the time so no harm was done except to the potatoes. At that point, I had enough. I called forth an Angel and asked what was going on. I assumed I had done something incorrectly to cause this to occur since Angels don't do those types of things to get your attention. The Angel said I didn't do anything to open up to this energy, it was my daughter. I went to my daughter and asked her what she did. She said that she hadn't done anything. The Angel said to ask her about the mirror. I knew about mirrors being spiritual windows and doorways so I asked her if she did anything in front of the mirror. She said a few days before she was worried about a history test so while she was brushing her hair she prayed for some help on her history test. She said the prayer in front of the mirror. At that point, I opened up my spiritual vision to that realm and I saw him. I asked what his name was and why he was in our home. He said his name was John Hancock and he was here to help my daughter with history. He said he knew a lot about history. I stuttered and said, "John Hancock; The John Hancock who signed the Declaration of Independence?" And he replied, "That's me." After I got over the shock, I told him he needed to leave. I felt his resistance and he stood there firmly in front of me. I asked the Angel why he could stay when I asked him to leave. The Angel told me that my daughter had opened the spiritual window so she would be the one that needed to get him back through it and close it behind him. I explained to my daughter what she had done and why those strange things were happening around our home. She agreed that she didn't want him there and would ask him to leave. She did but he was still resistant. So she got stronger in her tone and assured him that she would do fine in history and that she didn't need his help. He agreed to go and when I confirmed for her that he was gone, she went to the mirror and did what the Angel told her to do; she acted like she was closing a door. Then she made a cross of *light* over the mirror with her hand. Before I could say anything to her, she told me that she would never ask for any help in front of a mirror again.

Some of you might think that was fun. I didn't. And it ended up scaring my daughter. It was disruptive and lowered the energy of our home. He started throwing things around because he wanted me to notice him. After her history test, which she did very well on, he had nothing else to do but he still didn't want to leave.

I caution you to not try to bring anything through a mirror because there is a lot out there in Spirit and once they get in, it might be difficult to get them to leave. You might think you are calling forth someone particular but then you get someone else. There are so many other spiritual things to do to talk to people on the other side or get help; I would recommend never saying anything in front of the mirror. Please be cautious and wise in all spiritual matters.

MARIANNE AND NIKKI'S STORY ABOUT A DIMENSIONAL DOOR

I had a Soul Session with Christina and during the session I wanted to check in on my teenage daughter, Nikki. I have raised my kids to be very open and aware of the spiritual world and the fact that we are spiritual beings having a human experience and not humans having a spiritual experience and so they are very open. Nikki does have the ability to see spiritually. I don't see things the way she does as my strongest abilities are to hear and sense things. I have taught both of my children about the importance of being protected and they know if something is scaring them to call forth Archangel Michael. They know to surround themselves with his shield.

What I needed assistance with was that my daughter came to me telling me that she was seeing people and things in the hall in our home, especially at night. Sometimes this made her uneasy sometimes to the point where she didn't want to come out of her room. This had been going on for a couple of years.

Christina looked inside our house (spiritually) to see who was there. She found a spiritual doorway on the wall in our hall behind a picture of sea shells. She told me that she could help by closing the doorway so those in Spirit wouldn't be able to get in that way anymore. However, Christina saw that one of them was my daughter's grandmother. Her grandmother seemed to be worried about Nikki. Christina told me that if she closed that spiritual door, that would block the grandmother and everyone else in Spirit from coming in that way. And she said that it would upset Nikki's grandmother. If we leave the doorway open, others can come in. Christina didn't see that they were doing anything negative. They weren't trying to make noise. They were visiting because they could. Some of them don't have family on Earth that they could visit and so this is a fun thing for them to do. She shared with me that in spirit they could sense that we have a very high spiritual household and as such the area shines *light*, so they come to the *light*. Christina advised me to talk with Nikki to see what she would want to do about the spiritual doorway.

My sense was they aren't intending her harm (Christina confirmed that), it has been more her reaction to it and that is why I have been trying to work with Nikki. I kept saying to her that she had a wonderful gift and that she just needed to learn to work with it.

Christina explained that Nikki needs to know that she has control over any spiritual ability that she has. She can tell them to go away and most spirits will honor that request right away. But the problem is they would eventually come back. Unless we could figure out what the reason they were coming and take care of it, they would continue to come back. Now we understood our situation was a familial situation where Nikki was being watched over by her grandmother and that her grandmother was concerned about certain emotional situations that were going on. So it was out of her grandmother's love and concern that she was coming around. I found out her grandfather comes to visit also.

Christina could see a group that comes with the grandparents. Christina suggested that when Nikki saw them, she could say, "Thank you for being here but I want you to go away. You are making me uneasy. Come to me in my dreams because that would be much easier for me." Or she can say, "What is it that you want?" Christina explained that Nikki has the right to do this. We all do.

Christina also explained that when children are going through hormonal situations it tends to make those children who are spiritually open more intuitive. And sometimes they can get scared because they don't know what to do when they see a spirit walking around in their house. Christina said that Nikki was very comfortable with her abilities in spirit and she would grow into them. But this situation was bringing those abilities to the forefront a little earlier than Nikki's soul was expecting.

I did talk with Nikki about leaving the doorway open or having Christina close it permanently. She asked if the doorway could just be relocated somewhere else in the home, like downstairs. Christina said she couldn't do that because spiritual windows and doorways are not something that can be moved. They can only be opened or closed. These openings are not built like houses, they are where they are and then houses and buildings are built later. It would not matter if the house was torn down; the spiritual doorway was still going to be there because it does not exist in the physical realm.

I explained to my daughter that it could not be relocated -- that the options were to either close it off or leave it open. Then I reminded her that if Christina closed it off, her grandmother couldn't come in to the home. Nikki didn't want to do that.

Then Christina gave us another option. She explained that as child, she herself went through spiritual situations which caused a lot of uneasiness at that age too. She told me that just like her, Nikki could ask to stop her abilities. She could pray to not be able to see or hear those souls who are crossed over. What would happen is that her abilities would come back, like they did for Christina; hopefully giving her a few years of relief. Christina did this three times when she was growing up and then at 21 years old decided to find out why she had spiritual abilities and what to do with them. If Nikki did this, she would notice a difference immediately. Those in spirit would be able to visit except she would be oblivious to their presence.

Christina assured me that Nikki's abilities would not go away; they would come back. And Nikki could decide then if she was in a better position to start using them. And if not, she could ask for them to go away again. Eventually her soul would push the issue but as a child, she has plenty of time to connect to her full spiritual self.

We had three choices. We could have Christina close the spiritual doorway, Nikki could pray to have her abilities shut off for a while, or Nikki could decide to start learning more about her abilities. Nikki decided not to have Christina close the spiritual doorway because she didn't want to prevent her grandmother from visiting. She also didn't want to shut off her abilities. Instead she opted to work with her abilities with direction from Christina that she was in control of the situation. I think that just getting the explanation of what was going on and reinforcing what Nikki could do about the situation seemed to make her more comfortable with it.

REFRESHING YOUR SPIRIT

WHEN coming up with the information for this teaching, I had a wonderful, loving Angelic energy come into the room. She was very peaceful yet empowering. She was using that energy as a symbol of what happens when all of your chakras are opened and balanced. Having open and balanced chakras allows you to experience the true spiritual being that you are.

The first thing the Angels would like to acknowledge is our spiritual walk as human beings is not easy. Right now, we are holding in our aura the most energy that we ever have in any of our lives, at any time on Earth. That means that since we are in the third cycle of this Earth, we have attained more spiritual integration than in the first or second cycle of earth as well. So in this third cycle of Earth we are moving past the chains and bondage of ego more than ever before.

◄ YOUR DIVINE LIFE

In your spiritual walk things become disrupted in your life when you make the commitment to remember who you are and to develop your abilities. What you are doing is telling the Universe that you are ready to have this higher life and you are ready to release the things that hold you back. And in order to release them, you have to face them. The Angels have explained that it is not necessary for you to confront these things on the Earthplane; instead you can confront them spiritually and move past them for good. In the past, this is where we have had the most difficulty. We thought we had to deal with these things on the Earthplane, so we ended up taking the issues with us to our deaths, never releasing them and still holding them in our hearts.

The best thing you can do to aid your spiritual walk is to look at yourself; to look within your heart. Be honest with yourself as to what you are holding within your heart. If you are not sure what you are holding within your heart, listen to your speech. Listen to your speech 24 hours a day / 7 days a week. Your speech will tell you what is in your heart. If you are paying attention to the truth of who you are and how you are walking in this life then you will be able to identify the areas that you need to focus on. And you will be able to move more quickly into the areas of non-judgment, compassion and into a higher agape love, a God love for other people and humanity. It is not necessary for us to judge other people and see if they are walking in their truth; it is only necessary for us to look at ourselves.

I will guide you as to what prayers and affirmations to state for each chakra to help boost your spiritual walk to the highest level that you can be today. During this chakra work, you are going to notice several things. Sometime issues that we have will be linked to several chakras. For this exercise, we are going to be concentrating on the main chakra that has to do with that particular issue. The second thing you will notice is that everyone is your teacher and you are a teacher to everyone. It is sometimes difficult to recognize that in this life. You have at least one soul contract with someone in your life to act mean towards you, forcing you to be in difficult situations so that you can learn self-love. When you cross over you will see these same situations from a higher level and different perspective. I admit I do have a somewhat unique perspective from being a child who was able to assist the souls who were got lost when crossing over. I was able to go to the akashic records and see their lives. I was able to talk with these souls and find out why they were not moving on. This gave me the realization that there is a much bigger picture out there and when you grasp the bigger picture, you will be able to release these things in your life that are only holding you back. Releasing will allow you to be much lighter and happier and able to manifest the best and greatest for yourself. Because your soul will then be channeling more *light*, you will also be a blessing to every soul on the Earthplane today.

The Root Chakra is where we hold the past. When we become adults, we look at our childhood and we say, "Wow, I can't believe I made it through that. It was very difficult. So and so did this to me. And so and so did that to me." You move on in your life, think-

YOUR DIVINE LIFE

ing that you left all the issues behind. You think because you are an adult and you are not doing these same things to your family, children and friends, that you have moved past it. The Angels say that most of us are choosing not to think of the things in our past and ignore those old feelings. If your heart and mind continues to hold these negative issues, then less *light* can flow through you. It is important to release the past so that you can have your best life now. If you are still holding onto issues from before 2003 let it go; it no longer belongs to you. That is the other person you used to be before we made the shift to the 4th dimension. You can view it as a past life that you can clearly remember. It has nothing to do with your walk today and it is only making your path right now harder.

Thinking of that, place your hand two to three inches above your Root Chakra, which is at the bottom trunk of your body where you legs meet. Visualize *light* coming from your hand. (It will not really be coming from your hand, for those of you that can see the energy. It is coming from your heart. We use this technique to place the intention on where the *light* is to go.) Take a deep breath in and breathe out while visualizing the *light* going into the Root Chakra. State this with strong intention:

"I thank you, Archangel Michael for helping recognize where the past still has a hold on me. It is my intention to release the past now!"

Take a deep breath in; a deep cleansing breath drawing energy up from the Earth, really cleansing your body. And breathe out consciously releasing your past. Now take your hand and make a cross of *light* surrounded by a circle of *light* over the Root Chakra; sealing your intentions to release the past. Now take your hand and put it out in front of your mouth and blow into the palm of your hand to release that energy back to God. Shake your hand. Sometimes when I do this, I say the words, "The Breath of God" as I blow. By doing this, you are dissolving all of this energy into *light*. The Angels are saying that our intention is to put *light* through the palm of our hands into each chakra but because we are releasing energy and breaking through issues, some of that comes out and we are then transmuting that energy into the perfection of the breath of God. This does not happen to everyone for every chakra but they are teaching you the process and showing what you can do in your own practice.

Now we move onto the Sacral Chakra. This is the chakra where we hold and store energy when we feel we need protection. Most of the time when this chakra is out of balance, this energy is stored physically as fat. To assist with weight loss but also maintaining good health, the Angels want to remind everyone to bless your food to be exactly what you need at that time of the meal. If you are eating meat, bless the animal. If you are eating salad, bless the plants and vegetables. Thank the energy for being your sustenance for that meal. With this day and age of pesticides and all the things that are put onto and into our food, if you do this with belief and strong intention, you can eradicate any negative effects; you can raise the vibration to be exactly what you need for that meal. Remember we are very powerful beings, our intentions have power. You could say a prayer like this at each meal or over any snack:

"I thank You, Lord, that this food is exactly what my body needs right now. Anything more than my body needs is immediately released. I thank You that each animal or plant is blessed and thanked for its offering. Amen."

This is technically going to be a weight loss and / or balancing prayer. Now for this exercise, place your hand two to three inches above your Sacral Chakra, which is an inch or two below your navel. Visualize *light* coming from your hand into your chakra stating this with strong intention:

"I thank you, Archangel Metatron for showing me clear signs where I use food to cover my emotions. I want to be healthy and whole with my weight balancing at ____ pounds." Or if you are a perfect weight, then you can say this prayer for keeping that balance. The last line can be changed to: *"I want to be healthy and maintaining my current weight."*

Take a deep breath in, feeling that energy going into the Sacral Chakra. Breathe out, relaxing and feeling like you are a scale and you are balancing both sides of the scale perfectly. Now taking another deep breath in, make a cross of *light* surrounded by a circle of *light*. Taking your hand and put it in front of your mouth, blow any energy left on the palm of your hand back to God. Shake your hand.

We now move up to the Solar Plexus Chakra where you access your power. This is the strongest chakra that we have all experienced because it is the chakra which is tied to the 3rd dimension. When we planned this life, we were expecting to be in the 3rd dimension for our entire life. But in 2003, we moved to the 4th dimension by a collective Universal decision. And with that, the Solar Plexus Chakra needs to allow some of its energy to flow up to the 4th chakra so that the heart can be the strongest opening. Some people still feel butterflies in their stomach when they sense something is wrong. If you are experiencing this, you have too much energy flowing through your Solar Plexus. You are now supposed to be getting that sensation in your heart area because of our ascension to the 4th dimension. You don't want the concentration of your energy to be in your Solar Plexus anymore because that is the old, lower energy. With this next prayer we will be balancing this area.

The Angels want you to understand that from a very young age, you have been taught to accept being controlled. This has been taught to you lifetime after lifetime. There are hierarchies of family, work, government, etc. You have learned to give up your power. The Angels are here to help you get back your rightful power. No one can do anything to you that you do not allow. Now, we are not telling you to rise up against the government. We are telling you to look at things differently. Do not get upset at what you see or what you hear. Do not buy into negative things people are saying or you are hearing on the news. Don't buy into a recession. Do not buy into the control. Keep blinders on to all of the negativity and live to be a strong lighthouse of love and truth. This way you will affect other people in a positive way. If more than half of the souls here did this, there would be no need for government controls. It would just dissolve as there would be no need for anyone to tell us what to do. Remember, the government and other places of control are our teachers. They are catalysts for us to learn what we don't want to have in our lives. They are helping us to feel we deserve to have love and *light* in our lives.

There is no need to fear your own power either. In past lives and probably even this life, you have misused your power. It is an illusion that you are controlling other people. Everyone is playing a role in your life. If you are walking with integrity and truth, you will use your power in the highest and best way for the good of all. So there is no need to fear it. It is important for *Lightworkers*, *Lightbearers* and people integrating their spiritual-ness to use this power that they have. You cannot move forward to manifest miracles, canceling out diseases, or the down payment to your dream home without walking in your power and believing that you have a right to utilize it.

Put your hand two to three inches over your Solar Plexus, which is about an inch above your navel. Visualize the *light* coming from your hand. Remember intention is everything. Whatever your intention is, that is what will happen. Taking a deep breath in, state this prayer with strong intention:

*"I thank you, Archangel Uriel for helping me walk every day in the true power of who I came to be. I integrate my Earthplane walk with my spiritual life. I AM power walking in the *light*."*

Take a deep breath in with the intention of balancing your

Solar Plexus Chakra. Breathe out. Take in another deep breath making a cross of *light* with your hand surrounded by a circle of *light*. And breathe out. Taking your hand and put it in front of your mouth, blow any energy left on the palm of your hand back to God. Shake your hand.

Here we are now at the most important part of our 4th dimensional connection, the Heart Chakra. One of the blessings of the 4th dimension is a stronger opening to the Heart Chakra. In the 5th dimension, the opening to the Throat Chakra will be stronger. But we won't be able to have a stronger Throat Chakra if we are not opening our hearts to allow more *light* than ever before in our experience. Of course, the Heart Chakra is the area representing love. It is the most important chakra we have as physical beings because it is the connecting chakra between the lower physical chakras and the upper spiritual chakras. As such, it is an important part of your spiritual walk to check your heart. If your heart is blocked or closed due to unforgiveness, judgment or other lower energy, then you will be out of balance and some part of your life will not be going well.

If you ask to open your heart and take down any blocks or remove resistance to receiving love, you may notice some side effects. Your heart may flutter, you may be more emotional (tearing up or crying) or you may feel vulnerable. This may last for up to three days. How strong you feel these side effects will be equal to how strong the block you had over your heart. The Angels say it is like opening up the floodgate and after a little while you get control of the amount of water that is flowing through so the energy is handled better. At first, it can feel unusual; like a dam is bursting. The important thing is for you not to close your heart when you are feeling these things during those three days. If you ask to have your heart open and you end up feeling this way, take deep breaths and keep telling yourself these things:

- There is no need for the protection on your heart any longer.

- You are safe.

- You are secure.

- You know how to take care of yourself.

- Your Angels are there with you. If you need them, just call on them.

- All is well.

- In essence, what you are feeling is that you became a more empowered, spiritual human being by allowing more *light* to flow through you.

Placing your hand over your Heart Chakra with *light* flowing from the palm of your hand into your heart, state this with strong intention:

"I thank you, Archangel Raphael for helping me remove any

REFRESHING YOUR SPIRIT

blocks or protection I have over my heart. I recognize that everyone is my teacher and I AM no longer afraid to be me. I show the world who I truly am. I AM safe in your arms."

Take a deep breath in, allowing this love energy, this *light* to flow through your heart. And breathe out. Take another deep breath in. Make a cross of *light* surrounded by a circle of *light* and breathe out. Take your hand and breathe the energy off the palm of your hand sending it back to God.

At this point, you should be feeling pretty calm and peaceful and empowered from your legs up to your heart area. You should be feeling more energy flowing freely from the ground up than there is from the top down.

Now we will move up to your throat. Guess what the Throat Chakra deals with? Forgiveness! It is important to speak our forgiveness out loud. It is important for us to forgive ourselves for the things we feel we should have done better in our lives. And for the things that other people think we should have done better or differently which caused us to doubt ourselves and the decisions we have made. Also for the things that other people have done to us. And again, to recognize that all of these people and situations were placed in our lives to teach us and understand they are playing a role to help us be the best spiritual human being we can be. I know that especially in my life and from listening to people in their private phone Soul Sessions, people can be very mean to others, especially to loved ones. If you don't recognize the lesson

YOUR DIVINE LIFE

and you stay in that situation with these people, then your life can be pretty hard. That is why your Angels have brought you to this teaching. They want you to understand that if you are in a situation where you are being controlled and someone is teaching you how not to love, how to judge, how to control and you know this is not what you want any longer, there is help for you. The Angels are showing you an empowered way to release that energy and move past this lesson. You can forgive people from your past, even if they have already crossed over. You can forgive people currently in your life, even if you can't face them or don't want to face them and walk through this. This is the safest, highest, most loving way to forgive yourself and the other person.

Put your feet on the floor and take three long, slow, deep breaths. Call in your highest Angels simply by stating, "I want to talk with my highest Angels." Say, "I AM protected. I want to talk to _____ Angel." (State someone's name in there.) As you are breathing, tell the Angel everything that this person did to you. Say everything that you recognize now that you need to forgive and release. Forgive yourself for your part with this person. After you are done, thank the Angel and send the Angel back to the person. When that is done, your energy is severed from that person. This is not a time to be politically correct. This is a time to yell, cry, be angry, let out your frustrations for what could have been, etc. This empowers you by releasing all the feelings that have been stored up inside of your body. You are telling this person and the Universe that you want this cycle to end. Once you forgive, that higher energy goes out into the Universe clearing a higher path for you.

The Angels are saying that you are changing the cycle by forgiving that person and letting go of the energy and thanking them for being your teacher. You can also use this time with the Angel to tell the person that you don't want them in your life any longer or you can be specific and tell them that you don't want this energy and that you now do want them in your life but in a peaceful, loving relationship. You could state that you want to be able to attend a family party without backstabbing, gossiping, hurtful behavior, etc. You make that decision.

The other person's soul will receive the message within three days through the back door of their consciousness and heart. It does not confront their ego, which is what would happen if you were speaking to them in person. This way they always hear you. Three days is the amount of time that spiritual integration of messages is transmuted into the consciousness of a person on the Earthplane. (The example the Angels gave me is that it is the same amount of time that it took for Jesus Christ to come out of the tomb.) If you have issues with a parent, family member or a friend and you want things to change, that person always has a choice too. You can't make them do anything with this prayer. What you are doing is asking them in a clear, non-ego way through your heart what you would like. This creates loving energy for higher choices to be made. You have a great opportunity to have a happier life with these people if you let go of these issues that bind you through unforgiveness. Forgiveness is the key.

Remember to forgive yourself too! You did the best that you

could with the circumstances you were in and with the knowledge and wisdom that you had at that time. Unless you know how to time travel, you cannot go back to change it. Forgive yourself. Learn from it and move on. You are only hurting yourself by holding onto these issues and feelings. If you feel you did something to a person that could have been different, that person's life is not changed or helped by you feeling guilty. But you could be teaching that person that they too should feel guilty about things they do, which won't help them at all. This type of energy does not help or serve anyone.

Place your hand two to three inches over your Throat Chakra. Visualize *light* coming from the palm of your hand. State this with strong intention:

"I thank you, Archangel Gabriel for helping me forgive. I thank these people for being my teachers and I now choose to regain my power by releasing their energy from my life. They no longer have a hold on me."

Take a deep breath in. Breathe out, feeling your throat expand with *light*. Take a deep breath in placing a cross of *light* surrounded by a circle of *light* over your body. Breathe out. Taking your hand, blow the energy into the Breath of God and into the *light*. Shake out your hand.

Now we will move to the Brow Chakra which is sometimes known as the Third Eye Chakra. This is going to be a little bit different because this chakra deals with your spiritual connection and not your physical life lessons. We are going to be enhancing your connection to Spirit; your ability to see and hear and communicate spiritually. It is important for you to recognize that if your lower three chakras are not in balance, it is very difficult to connect to Spirit. Some people may think that concentrating on the upper, more spiritual chakras will help them advance quicker. The opposite is true. Being grounded to earth makes it easier to reach up higher into the dimensions. So the advice is to give the same amount of attention to all the chakras.

So with a spiritual connection, you are able to communicate with your higher self, those who are crossed over, beings in other dimensions and the Angelic realm. You can choose who you talk to and at what level. Your Brow Chakra is your connection point to being able to do so. I have chosen to connect with the realm of the Angels or above. I have learned in my spiritual teachings that the Angels have a higher perspective on where we are on the Earthplane and what our individual purpose is while we are here. They are here to help us in our lives. You make your own choice and you can always choose different places / beings at different times. To be proficient, it is advised you work with one level at a time until you are skilled with that level and then you can move on. But there is no right or wrong here. It's just that some beings are easier for us to deal with.

Spiritual sight is from within, so there is no need to fear. When you get a vision, it is like a dream or a memory. Very few people enjoy seeing spiritual beings outside of themselves with their physical eyes. This is a soul's choice. I have seen that way a couple of times and it scared me! So I prayed never to see like that again And I never have. There really is no need to see people who are crossed over in the physical realm. You can just as easily get whatever message or help them by seeing them inside your head. My spiritual sight comes from within me and I wouldn't have it any other way. If you want to see a vision, you can close your eyes and direct your eyes upward and inward to look in between your eyebrows. See a blank screen and ask the Angels to show you their messages there.

What we are going to do is to open your Brow Chakra one more layer than where it is right now. Placing your hand two to three inches above your Brow Chakra, which is in between your eyebrows at the bridge of your nose. Visualize *light* flowing from the palm of your hand. State this with strong intention:

"I thank You, Holy Spirit for opening my spiritual eyes to see the bigger picture of my walk here on Earth. I want to communicate with the Angels in my daily life. I AM ready to move to the next level of my spiritual development."

Take a deep breath in. And breathe out. This time, take your hand, moving it like you are scraping away one layer over your Brow Chakra. (Remember you are not actually touching your skin; the chakra resides our a few inches from your body.) Take a deep breath in, placing your hand back over your new Brow Chakra and make a cross of *light* surrounded by a circle of *light*. Breathe out. Take your hand and place it in front of your mouth breathing the excess energy back to God. Blow that energy into the *light*. Shake out your hand.

The Crown Chakra is usually open if your heart is open. When you start to move into the higher lessons of your Crown Chakra, things can get a little tough in your daily walk. You will meet the most unloving people, who are there to teach you not to judge. You will meet people who want your help but who are not willing to do the things you or Spirit suggests will help them. This is where non-judgment comes in. In these higher lessons, you are learning to love people enough to allow them to walk their own walk. If they come to you and they want something, then you share with them whatever you feel you should. But when they leave, let them go out of your thoughts. It is not your responsibility for you to follow up with them. The next time you see them, it is not for you to ask them if they did what you had suggested. The one area that is difficult for me is my husband and my children. That seems to be the case for most people because usually at this point, we have already separated from our birth families but we still feel we can "save" our significant other and children. You have done so much work on yourself and you want your family to have the best, easiest life. That is understandable but it is not the higher spiritual path. We recognize you don't want them to go through what you went through. But you should be able to recognize that they are not where you are at on their spiritual path and they may not understand what you are talking about. Sometimes your loved ones will be polite and listen to you. Then they go off and do their own thing despite what wisdom you have shared. So when you get to these higher lessons, it is important for you not to get frustrated and to understand that their Angels are working with them too. You may try telling them these things you have learned one, two or three times and then the fourth time; you need to recognize they don't want to hear this. So let it go. You then have a choice to be there when they recognize they now need your help because they didn't take the higher road in whatever situation they were going through. If you decide that you are not going to be there for them at that time that is fine. There are a lot of teachers, healers, people who are blaming themselves for their clients not being healed, emotionally or physically or not moving on spiritually in their abilities. They may have drug or sexual issues, or disease issues, etc. You recognize that healing techniques like Reiki and the *light* can help them but you see the person laying there suffering because they won't accept it. And you feel you have to convince them to have the healing session. If they cross over, you might feel guilty that you were not able to talk them into it. The Angels are saying that you are taking on way, way too much responsibility! That is not the highest place for you to be because you are placing a judgment on yourself to take the responsibility of what that soul wanted to do. Every soul has an opportunity to walk in the *light* and accept a higher, easier path. If they don't accept it from you, maybe you were just the first layer of the experience for them. If they do accept it from you, maybe you were the tenth person that had contact with them to integrate this knowledge and energy. You might think it was a miracle that in your first contact, they were healed. But in reality, nine other people had laid the foundation for the person to accept a higher walk in life. It finally clicked at this point and (egotistically) you are taking the credit. The Angels are stating that you need to be detached with clients and perhaps with your friends and family if you are sharing information with them and trying to help them. You are to be there for the people who are ready. You will be prompted when people need your help. But it is up to them whether they accept your or Spirit's information or any healing. Then have no attachment to the results. If they come back to you and say, "You didn't heal me." Your ego is not going to rise up and try to defend yourself. You understand that was their choice. However, it is always good to check to see where you were at spiritually when you did the healing. If you were the highest and clearest channel you could be for that person, there is nothing for you to be concerned about or change in your healing practices. On the other hand if they come to you and say, "You healed me." You acknowledge that you were just the channel for the healing and you rejoice that the soul accepted the highest and easiest path. It is always a joyous occasion when a soul chooses the easy path!

As weird as it may sound, some people do not want to be healed. Some people whom we love very much want to be miserable. You may not want to live that way. That is why you are taking the steps to help yourself. Looking back at your life, how many people tried to help you when you were not ready to hear? This area of your Crown Chakra is about non-judgment and walking in non-attachment. We are releasing judgment of the choices other people make; how and why they do the things that they do. You will feel a weight lift off of you if this where you are having issues.

Place your hand two to three inches above your Crown Chakra, which is above your head and move the hand an inch to the back. Visualize *light* coming from your hand and state this with strong intention:

*"I thank You, Christ Light for helping me see a more spiritual perspective of life on Earth. I am asking for you to help me to hold my tongue when I am in judgment. Then I ask Your help to have me recognize my judgmental thoughts and to release them. My intention is to walk in the highest love and *light* now!"*

Take a deep breath in. And breathe out. Take a deep breath in and make a cross of *light* surrounded by a circle of *light*. And breathe out. Take the energy in your hand and breathe it back to God. This dissipates any excess energy into the *light*. Shake out your hand.

When you open up your chakras and you have released unforgiveness from your heart, when you strive to walk in love and in *light*, just being the best that you can be, you all of a sudden stop living in the past. The very next thing that happens is you stop anticipating the future. Things start happening in the now. Living in the now, you manifest things exactly as you need them.

Here is a personal example of living in the now. My husband

went to the post office and called me saying that he couldn't start the car. He asked me to come get him. When I got there he said the problem was the battery. So I ran into the post office, grabbed my mail and then we went to the auto store to get a new battery. When he was inside, I opened up the mail. When he got back in the car, I asked how much the battery was and he said $70. I handed him the envelope I received in the mail and it was a money order for $70. Living in the now, I had no fear after his phone call that I wouldn't have money for whatever the car needed, even though we had no extra money in our bank account. I trusted that all would be provided for and it was. That is only one of many things that happen to me daily because I live very expectantly that all of my needs will be provided for. If I do get into fear about something, I try to recognize it and then I ask the Angels for help in releasing the fear and then move on with my day not dwelling on it. It is a wonderful way to live! If you keep your chakras open and you do these things that we are sharing they can change your life!

Now we are going to move back to the heart area. When you open up all of your chakras, you open up your heart even more. This is because you have *light* coming from Mother Earth through your lower chakras and you have the "light" from Heaven coming down and funneling all of this *light* energy into your heart. And then it explodes out of your heart. This is not creating an imbalance because there is so much energy. Instead, in this way it is very balanced. 4th dimensionally, it is appropriate for that much energy to be flowing into and out of the Heart Chakra. This energy is helping you to experience compassion, which is one of the highest things we can experience in this life other than agape love. Agape love is the God love without judgment, without control, without guilt, without worry. He loves us just because we exist. He loves you just the way you are today and that is what we can experience when this back door to our heart opens. You can be an open, flowing, balanced being of pure spiritual *light*.

Place your hand back over your heart and experience this compassion. State this with strong intention:

"I thank you, my dear highest Angels for helping me to this stage in my spiritual walk. I now have eyes to see the truth without fear. I use my truth each day to be a balanced spiritual human being. Please help me when I stumble or forget and show me clear signs of your presence every day. I thank you for your never failing love, your guidance and your protection."

Take a deep breath in and visualize a door opening to your heart. It can be a single door or double doors. Place your hand over your heart with *light* flowing from your palm. Visualize these doors opening out towards your hand from the back of your heart. And you are pouring *light* into that doorway. Breathe out. Take another deep breath in and seal that door open with a cross of *light* surrounded by a circle of *light*. Breathe out. How do you feel? How does compassion feel? Do you feel peaceful? Do you feel love? Do you feel loved? Do you feel complete? You can have this feeling anytime. Just remember to focus your attention on your heart and breathe deep.

LISA'S STORY

I feel incredibly blessed that I have met Christina and received the information that she taught me and my family regarding how the Angels can assist us in our everyday lives by remembering all we have to do is ask.

In May of 2003, my younger brother Michael died in a car accident just one mile from home. He was only 23 years old. My family was absolutely devastated. My brother, Bob was so upset that he never had the chance to say goodbye and really wanted a sign from Michael that he was okay. After the burial, our family all retreated to my mother's home. It was a beautiful day and we were outside visiting with relatives we have not seen for years. While reminiscing about our memories of Michael, a neighbor called to tell us to look outside at the golf course across the street. There was a beautiful rainbow above on a day where there were no storms and only blue skies. I immediately ran to get my brother Bob, showing him the rainbow and declaring that this must be the sign he asked to receive letting us know that Michael was fine and for us not to worry about him. Michael was an avid golfer and spent much of his time on that golf course, so that sign was very significant to us and we did not think of it as a coincidence.

Several months later in October (near Michael's birthday of

October 28), a friend of mine asked me to go with her to an Angel seminar at a local Healing Arts Center. I was quite curious and yet nervous at the same time. I always believed in Angels, but was uncertain about what an Angel Channeler was or actually did. I decided to go. Christina told us about her background and how she started working with Angels. She taught us that Angels want to assist us with anything, no matter how big or small the issue. All we had to do was ask and they were more than willing to help. Later in the seminar she explained that the Angels would channel through her and provide the group with a message and then we could ask specific questions about anything we wanted to know about our lives. I was intrigued. When the Archangels introduced themselves and gave their special message, I noticed they spoke through Christina in a calm, soothing demeanor. They gave a global message and some specific messages. Then they allowed everyone to ask a question of their own that pertained to their life. I was quite overwhelmed and in awe, and when it was my turn, all I could say was, "Who sent the rainbow?" That was all I had to say, as they knew exactly what I was referring. They explained that only God could send a rainbow and my brother had asked to send one as a sign that he was just fine. They explained that it is hard for those who are still here on Earth to understand why someone so young is gone before they think it is their time. They explained that everything is part of a larger, divine plane and that Michael was doing just fine and was very happy. This was very comforting to me and I was very excited to tell my family what the Archangels told me.

After the seminar, I could not stop thinking about what I had learned from the Angels. One day while I was at work, I reached into my purse for a pen and a piece of paper stuck to my finger. It was a handout from the Angel seminar with Christina's contact information, saying that she does group and private sessions and that we could ask anything about our life, career, finances, or deceased loved ones. I thought that it was odd that it stuck to my finger, so I folded it up and placed it back in my purse. I turned back to my computer and started working. Just then a song on the radio caught my full attention. It was an old song from the 80's with the lyrics, "How do you talk to an Angel."

I remembered from the seminar that Christina said that if the Angels want to get a message to you they will keep trying. First was the paper from the seminar sticking to my finger, then the song. I immediately called my mom and asked if I should ask Christina to come over to my house when she, my brother, my grandmother, and aunt and uncle would be in town visiting me in Florida from Pennsylvania. I told her I had a strong notion that this may have something to do with Michael and him wanting to get a message to all of us, since it would be around his birthday. This would be his first birthday after his death and we were still very much grieving him. My mom was definitely interested in it, since she had recently spoken with a psychic who had given her accurate feedback about Michael and his energetic spirit. I immediately contacted Christina and scheduled a group session for our family.

On the day of the session, we wrote down our questions before Christina arrived at my home. Once she was there, she gave an overview of the Angels and then we were able to ask our questions. Our first question was, "Who was responsible for gathering us here today?" The Angels said it was Michael. He was here with us. He wanted us there together to explain that he was okay and that he needed us to send him the *light* when instead we felt like grieving for him. They explained that when we are upset and thinking about him, that he would stop what he was doing in spirit and come to be with us. He could be at different places at the same time, since time did not exist on the other side where he was. However, this required much energy. His purpose at that time was to assist children who were crossing over. He was helping them to understand what was happening to them. Surely, we wanted to assist him, so we were going to try our best to send him the *light* when we thought of him and especially when we were sad and grieving.

We got all of our questions answered which made us feel more connected. We were happy to find out that he was greeted when he crossed over by our deceased loved ones, especially my grandfather, who the Angels said spends a lot of time with Michael. My grandmother had smiled and was grateful for this information.

I also noticed the incredible effect the Angels had on the dogs and cat during Christina's visit. Before she started her session, I had asked her if I should put the animals in the other room, since I thought animals could sense spirits and might bark or meow throughout the session. Christina told us that the Angels had a calming effect on animals. They surely did! My cat, which is not fond of visitors, came

REFRESHING YOUR SPIRIT

out and rubbed up against Christina then laid in the middle of the floor for all to see her. My dog jumped up on the couch where I was sitting and laid her head on my lap and stayed there the whole time. And my grandmother's dog, which typically is very hyper, jumped up on the couch and lay in between my mom and me and did not move the entire time. It truly was amazing!

Christina also explained that if we knew of someone who was sick or going through a hard time that we should send them the *light*, too. At that time, we all sent the *light* to my husband's baby nephew, who was in the hospital with the outcome not looking good. He had become very sick one evening and was airlifted from one hospital to another for emergency surgery where half of his colon had to be removed. A few hours after sending baby Adam the *light*, my husband received a call that the baby opened his eyes for the first time and his condition was rapidly improving. It was a miracle! I am happy to report that Adam is quite an active toddler today. We were amazed and thankful!

There was one more awesome occurrence the day Christina came to share with us that caught our attention. After Christina left, our family went out to dinner to celebrate my Aunt's birthday. We went to a Japanese steakhouse where the chef prepares the meal in front of you in an entertaining fashion. We gasped when our chef came out. He was not wearing the normal white chef hat, instead it was a material design that we were familiar with. It was a pattern of red, orange and yellow flames. He was also wearing a tie to match the tall chef hat. This was a clear message for us to receive at that time. My Aunt had worn my brother's shirt which had this exact flame pattern on his birthday a few weeks earlier to honor him. We were now celebrating her birthday that day, so we truly believe that he was letting her know that he appreciated what she did on his birthday and also for us all learning about the Angels. The ultimate message was that he was okay and he was with us!

Since then, my family has relied on the Angels in our everyday lives and has experienced wonderful assistance! We share our stories with our many friends and other family members, and have occasionally heard feedback of how the Angels have assisted them. It is comforting to know the Angels are with us and will help us at any time with anything!

MATILDA

A SPIRITUAL DOG-NAPPING

WE adopted Matilda from a family who couldn't keep her anymore. She looks like a Tibetan terrier but is actually a large Cockapoo. She was healthy and happy for about 3 years. Then one day while she was sleeping in front of the fireplace by herself she had a grand mal seizure. We had never experienced anything like that before. It was horrible and we felt so helpless while she was going through it. We took her to the vet and he gave her some phenol barbital, which knocked her out for just a short while and stopped the seizure. The vet advised us on what to do if and when she had future seizures and what to look out for if they got worse. It was good that we had the information because she had seizures on a regular basis after that. I kept praying for an answer as to what was going on and how this happened.

My answer came in a dream (vision) about a young girl who came through a spiritual dimensional doorway which was in our fireplace. She had tried to pull Matilda through the spiritual doorway. I was so surprised that I immediately woke up. Was this possible? Could this have started because of a spiritual kidnapping attempt? I asked a friend what I should do with the information from the vision. Was it really an answer or was it just a dream? She said I needed to request that my Angels take me to the dimension where this girl was and ask her why she was trying to take our dog, if this was what really happened. I did ask them. And they did assist me with going to her dimension. During the first attempt, I noticed I could see the girl and my house just as it was but I couldn't make any connection with her. I asked my Angels why it wasn't working and they said I was nervous and stressed so I really hadn't traveled anywhere. I tried again. This time I relaxed and breathed deep but tried to stay as conscious as possible instead of doing this in my sleep because of the seriousness of the situation.

This time I saw her and I knew she saw me. She was about nine years old. I knew her name was Carrie. Carrie was calling for her dog right outside what looked like a duplicate of our house. I asked her what she was doing. She said she had lost her dog but had recently found him. She was trying to get him to come back home with her. I told her she was mistaken and that Matilda was a female not a male and she was our dog. Carrie was stubborn and said it was her dog and she was going to take it back home with her. I had no experience with this kind of situation and didn't know what to do! So I called forth an Angel and asked the Angel to assist her with finding her dog. (It was the only thing I could think of!) The Angel agreed. I told her that if she went with the Angel he would help her to find her dog; the right dog. She was reluctant but after a few minutes of coaxing, she went with the Angel.

I was relieved and thought everything was going to be put back the way it was before she made this spiritual kidnapping attempt. I was wrong. Matilda's seizures were increasing; soon she was having multiple seizures one after the other. She was exhausted. We took her to the vet and he said we should put her to sleep because she wouldn't live any kind of life on the medicine it would take to control the seizures. The medicine would eventually wear her liver out so she would only have a year or two left anyway. We just couldn't accept that and took her home and decided not to take her back to the vet.

I talked with the Angels and asked them why she was still having the seizures after I had taken care of the source of the problem. They said that when she was being pulled through the dimensional doorway, damage was done to her aura which then caused damage to parts of her brain. She resisted so much that her body stayed here in the physical but part of her spirit got through. At the time Carrie was originally trying to take her, we had heard Matilda screaming so we went to help her. I didn't realize what was going on spiritually but I do feel now that by talking to her we helped her stay in this dimension with us. If the young girl had been successful in taking her, we would have found Matilda's dead body by the fireplace and not known what had happened. What we were dealing with now was that Matilda's aura was torn and the physical damage was already in the cells. The brain remembered how to have a seizure so it was just continuing on the path that it thought it was supposed to go on. (This happened ten years before Jesus showed me how to heal these issues.)

I pressed the Angels for an answer to help her. There had to be a way to fix this. Matilda didn't ask for this to happen to her. And I knew it wasn't a lesson for her as animals are not on Earth to learn lessons like we are. I was guided by the Angels to do a search on the internet for dog seizures. The Angels showed me an obscure study that was done with dogs that had seizures and the success with using herbal supplements and cell salts. Going to the health food store, the Angels showed me which two cell salts to give to Matilda and gave me the dosage. They also guided me to give her Valerian root to calm her nerves, which were basically fried at this point. The good news is that Matilda never had another seizure after that day. Every day for five years we gave her the cell salts and Valerian root, changing amounts as I was guided. One day out of the blue, the Angels told me she didn't need them anymore. We gradually weaned her off the supplements. That was four years ago as I write this and we are happy to report she is still seizure free.

I wrote this prayer/poem the night of her last seizure praying for her to be healed:

"Dear God of Power and Might,

Please be with us during this night

For our dog, Matilda which we hold dear

Is seizure bound and we need that cleared.

Matilda has recently been very sick

But we know you have been with us through thin and through thick.

Your comforting, healing *light*

Is just what she needs this very night.

And in the morning when we wake

We will remember what was at stake.

And give You praise and glory

For Your promises are not just stories.

For Matilda has been healed;

The sickness had to yield

To the All Powerful and Glorious Might

Of the One I AM, the God of day and night."

Much later I received insight into why some people and animals have epileptic and grand mal seizures. When you are seeing someone you love go through this, it makes no sense. What could possibly be the purpose of something so uncontrollable? The answer I received was beautiful. These people and animals who have these seizures are sacrificing themselves to be channels for disruptive energy. When they come across unbalanced, unsettled energy, they can have a seizure which accepts the disruptive energy into their body and clears it out of the room or area. They literally absorb the energy into their body, which causes the seizure and then allow this energy to flow through their aura to go into the *light*. After the energy is cleared, the seizure is over. Unfortunately, this is very hard on the physical body. They willingly maintain energetic balance. There are people and animals that have chosen to do this as their service to humanity. They are called *Lightbearers* and they are very powerful souls. (Not all *Lightbearers* can do this.) This wasn't the case for our Matilda but since I was asking so many questions about seizures and received this information, I wanted to pass it along to you.

MICHAEL

A LABOR DAY SURPRISE

ON the Friday before Labor Day, my husband decided to go to Home Depot to pick up some tools. When he walked to get in his truck, he thought he heard a soft, "Meow." He opened the door to the truck and then heard it again. He walked to the front of the truck and heard the meowing coming from under the hood. So he opened up the hood of the truck and saw a little kitten. The kitten was stuck in the driver's side wheel well. He had to get under the truck to get the kitten out. The kitten was small enough to fit in the palm of his hand.

When we got the kitten inside we noticed a momma cat walk into our yard and look into the window at us and then go over to the truck to make sure we had the kitten. We walked out with the kitten but she turned and ran away and never came back. I knew then she had placed the kitten there on purpose.

At that time we were a dog family. We had never owned cats, thought of owning cats or wanted to own cats. Since it was late in the day on Friday we realized that we were going to be taking care of the kitten until at least Tuesday because Monday was Labor Day.

We weren't sure how the dogs would respond to a kitten so we introduced them one by one. The kitten was very small and looked like it was a week old. The dogs all licked it and seemed to understand the plight of this kitten.

All through the weekend, my family was in agreement that on Tuesday we would give him to someone who actually wanted a kitten. Instead on Tuesday, we were guided to take her to our vet. In the few days we had taken care of the kitten, we had already fallen in love. It was then that we got the news. The first was that he was actually a she. The vet estimated her age at two weeks old. Then the bad news; she had feline leukemia. The vet suggested that since he didn't think we had any emotional attachment to the kitten in that short time period, he could put her to sleep right then. Immediately, we all said, "No." By spending the weekend with her, we had already decided to keep her and that the mother cat must have given her to us for a reason. He informed us that she would only live a month or possibly two with as advanced as the leukemia was.

MICHAEL

We took her home and decided to name her Michael, even though she was a female, because we knew she needed the strength of Archangel Michael to survive. I had already learned that names were powerful. So we figured every time we spoke to Michael by invoking that name, she would get stronger. We all joined our thoughts and prayers to ask for guidance on the highest ways to take care of her.

I thought it was going to be a big difference having a kitten. But it wasn't hard at all. Michael basically showed us how to take care of her. What we didn't perceive from her logically, I received from her spiritually. We knew she was delicate and were concerned about the dogs but every day we saw her curled up beside one of the dogs. They were all careful when she was around. A few months later, she was eating out of the dog bowls at their dinner time and refused all cat food. She would run and jump and play. The dogs really understood that they could hurt her so they were always very gentle. It was amazing to see!

We never went back to the vet and spent over two years with her. When she crossed over, she had only shown signs for a couple of days of needing more warmth than usual (so we would warm up a towel for her to lie on) and wanting to sleep more. I kept asking spiritually if she wanted us to help her cross over just like I had been doing regularly all through this time with her and she always answered the same, "No." We made her as comfortable as possible and she died in my husband's loving arms. We never knew how a little kitten would change our lives! Oh how we loved

Michael! We thanked her for allowing us to be the ones to have a life with her and prayed that she would return to us in a cat that was physically healthy and strong with the strength of Michael as soon as possible.

EINSTEIN

OUR KITTEN REINCARNATED

A year later, I went to Einstein's Bagels Restaurant to get breakfast. On this particular day, there were people from a local animal shelter outside with the pets they had available for people to adopt. I walked by the animals in the cages, not even imagining for a moment that an hour later I would be taking one of them home. After breakfast, I had to walk past them again and someone noticed that when I walked by one of the kittens came to the front of the cage and stuck it's paw out to me. And when I was away, he went to the back of the cage as if to hide. I thought that was crazy so I purposely walked by. Sure enough, he came to the front as if he knew me. I looked at him and thought he looked familiar but couldn't put my finger on it. I felt a strange pull in my heart as I called my husband and asked if I could bring home a kitten. At that point, we had four dogs and two cats. This would make a total of seven animals not counting the saltwater fish and an eel. He surprised me by saying "Yes." But he continued by telling me that if I got any more animals he was going to put a sign up in the front yard that would say "Christina's Ark!" I filled out the paperwork, paid and took the kitten home. I named him Einstein after the restaurant where I found him. It wasn't until we got home that we realized that Einstein looked exactly like Michael. He had the same facial markings, he was the same color and he seemed to know all of us. He even ate the same way Michael did out of the dog bowl at dinner time. Einstein did many things to show us that he was Michael. Einstein has been a healthy cat with an extremely strong personality. We all agree, he is definitely Michael reincarnated. And we are thankful!

FINAL THOUGHTS

AS an Ambassador of the Christ energy, I am here to share with you messages of truth, *light*, knowledge and wisdom. Hopefully, the messages in this book assisted by giving you a greater understanding of how to personally connect to your Angels (Soul), how to be a balanced spiritual human being and how to go through the Ascension in the easiest way. I pray these messages were empowering for you. It is not an easy task to remember the full spiritual being you are. Your Angels will assist you as long as you remember to ask for their help and guidance. As we continue to remember more, we will hold more *light* within our beings. We will be able to do more to help ourselves, help others and Mother Earth. We have to go through this experience on Earth because we asked for it. What we are being reminded is that we have a choice in how we go through it. If you feel you want to make some changes in your life, start today. Why wait for the life that you deserve? Call forth your Angels daily, be more conscious of the words you are speaking in to your life and remember how important it is to forgive. In this book and through our teachings, we have given you many powerful tools to assist you to be as strong as you are ready to be. Through these tools, you will also be clearing the way for the next level of life on Earth, the 5th dimension; otherwise known as the Christ Consciousness. The fullness of that dimension being anchored on Earth is rapidly approaching. Be ready to step over into the 5th dimension by getting prepared now.

My prayer for you is that you now experience the joy in your life today that you so richly deserve and that you accept the blessings that have been waiting for you. Thank you for the honor of allowing me to serve you in this way!

Many Blessings of Joy,

Christina

"This is what was spoken by the prophet Joel:

And it shall come to pass in the last days, says God

That I will pour out My Spirit on all flesh;

Your sons and your daughters shall prophesy,

FINAL THOUGHTS

Your young men shall see visions,

Your old men shall dream dreams.

And on My menservants and on My maidservants

I will pour out My Spirit in those days;

And they shall prophesy."

~ Acts 2:16 – 18

ARCHANGEL CHAKRA PRAYER

"All chakras opened and blessed

To receive the full integration of *light*

So that I AM a pure and clear channel

And the full spiritual being

Exemplifying the Christ Consciousness

That I came here to be!"

FOR MORE INFORMATION ABOUT:

- Christina's spiritual work

- Private Soul Sessions with Christina

- To sign up for monthly Angel Messages

- To watch videos of The Archangel Chakra Prayers and Soul Teachings

- Free monthly Soul Teachings by phone

- To have Christina come to teach and share in your city, state or country or at an event

- Christina's Book: <u>The Angel Connection; Divinity in the New Energy</u>

- Christina's Soul Teachings on CD

Please visit her website at:
www.CreatorMediator.com

CPSIA information can be obtained at www.ICGtesting.com
Printed in the USA
BVOW040917121011

273447BV00001B/5/P

9 781432 74122